Poetry of Life

Jitendra Ratansinh Raol, Ph. D.

Trafford PUBLISHING®   www.trafford.com

North America & international
toll-free: 1 888 232 4444 (USA & Canada)
phone: 250 383 6864 ♦ fax: 250 383 6804 ♦ email: info@trafford.com

Our task must be to free ourselves - by widening our circle of compassion to embrace all living creatures and the whole of nature and its beauty - Albert Einstein

Whether God exists or not, whether we believe in him/her or not, we do exist. In short span of our lives on this planet, what perhaps best we can feel and experience is the Godhood-of-Love and spread its message to entire humanity-JIRARA

Dedicated to

My mother, sister, wife, daughter and two grand daughters and in loving memory, to my two grandmothers

Poetry of Life

Preface

Poems originate in our heart, a metaphor for the mind. Then sailing on the waves of our mind (thoughts) the poetry gets into motion. And, perhaps, with a feather touch of some wisdom of our emotional intelligence and a bit of spiritual intelligence, the poems get written down. The poems in this book are about people and places, their ups and downs, about phenomena I have observed and dreamt. Most poems are of reflective nature: about life and its events that surround us. We take up the challenges and pose ourselves to these events with dedication, determination, devotion and duty with sacrifices as many as we can make. These events mould our minds, rekindle our thoughts and refine our wisdom with new spirit to face more complex problems already waiting for us on our path to the so called 'self-realization'. Isn't life a serious business! May be yes, may be not! An attempt is made to bring in some poetry in life in this book. It would be useful to first read the notes and glossary. In first reading of the book, the 'Seek Almighty' may be skipped. A few poems (some are prose-like) would amuse, some would prompt a self-analysis and some would inspire. Some have more than one shade of meaning and interpretation - left to the imagination of the reader and her/his background, experiences and feelings. If any of the foregoing happens then some purpose of 'Poetry of Life' would have been served.

- JIRARA (Author)

Acknowledgements

Several teachers from my schooling and college days and years have helped me shape my thoughts in the directions wherefrom I experienced many beautiful relationships and bonds with people, places and events of life. My dedicated and very affectionate father provided a fair and just background for me to read books on philosophy from his cupboard-library. He gave me abundance of opportunities to grow and experiment. My mother Trikamkunwarba, wife Virmati, son Mayur and daughter Harshakumari gave me tremendous moral support during my very difficult times and psychological ordeals. Many close relatives, friends, and colleagues showed total affection and gave moral support for all these years. Specifically Ms. Radhika and Dr. Mrs. Girija have been wonderful human beings and friends who have been and are my all-time well wishers. I am personally grateful to my daughter-in-law Gayathri for bringing an initial excitement, innocence and beauty in our house-family-home. I am also very grateful to my son-in-law Hitendrasinh and his family for adhering to the beautiful bonds of family relations. If any thing went wrong with anybody (including myself), the responsibility lies with me. I stand corrected. I hope the greater life would forgive me. Health of my all the family members, including myself was surcharged by the excellent doctors: Dr. K. S. Nanjudaswamy, Dr. Pranesh, Dr. Mrs. K. Lalitha, Dr. Amaranarayan, Dr. Ramakrishna, and Dr. Mrs. Swetha

Desai. Dr. Rajpuriya has been our excellent family doctor for many years from my childhood days.

The excellent literature/discourses from Swami Chinmayanandji, Swami Dayanand Saraswathiji, Shree Shree Ravishankarji, Swami Sukhbodhanandji, Prof. Isaac Asimov, and Prof. Richard Dawkins have been encouraging, inspirational and very useful to me.

-JIRARA

1. A barefooted farmer boy

I saw you ploughing bare footed on black soil
one treacherous hot afternoon
while on a pleasure trip in a train
to my native town.

The pasty layers of the soil under
your feet were your only soles
while you worked in unison with the open blue sky
to transform the black hard gold
into green farms.

To provide grains for millions
to quench their hunger
while you plough ceaselessly on the black soil
under hot Sun braving dusty winds
You, barefooted farmer boy.

2. Innocent bride – A prelude to Birth of a mother

Far from the urban hassles in a small village
brought up in midst of ignorance and dust
full of buoyant innocence
unaware of vagaries of life's uncertain future.

But in the din of a town far from the village dust
her destiny awaited her arrival
in the midst of rules and conventions
burden of realities of routines and chores.

Suddenly the life comes to a dead spell
future shrinks with a lightening stroke
lashes of law of 'Karma' on the back
far from the sweet home in the close cell of widowhood.

Undreamt, untold miseries
struck the innocent unprepared
brought up naturally in the midst of the nature
yet to be hit by the nature's law of 'Karma'- action!

3. Birth of a mother

Dressed in bright colorful silk saari
with my body laden with gold ornaments, bathed in perfume
when I, as a young bride, entered the bedroom of my husband
succumbed in the embrace of the man in his late fifties
the fire engulfing the yester years' playful childhood.

The roamings in the mountainous valleys
memories of splashing in cold waters of the rivers
the sands and dusts, green farms and water falls
all resurrected on the plane of my mind
in the darkness of the night
and brightness of the fire of the desire.

The images of the chirping birds and the grazing cows, buffalos
my ramblings in the dreams to be in a town or a city
to feel the vastness and greatness of the new places and peoples
started flying away like the ashes
with the onslaught at its peak.

The body union transformed my dreams and joy
into the chores of the daily life
sweeping the floors of the old house, feeding grass to the cattle
igniting earthen fire-places and feeding numerous guests
as a part of the service to the God of my new life.

Afternoons of occasional small naps
the evenings of the waiting for my lord
who wanted me to beget his own son
for he did not have one from his previous wives
who left nothing behind to cherish by him.

His eyes wanted more of my beauty, and charm
his desire more of my flexible body, and tenderness
and my obedience to say yes to all his requirements
paid-off one fine day and Lo! I gave birth to a male baby.

Soon the clouds gathered by the storm
the darkness laid down its carpet and the inevitable happened
my old man slept a silent sleep for ever leaving me behind
with my only son who did not know meaning of life and death.
And soon stripped of my
beautiful ornaments and dreams
dressed in the garments of a widow
amongst the relatives mourning for the gone old man
I resumed the routine vagaries of another phase of my life with
tonsured head and display of courage as
the newly borne mother of my new baby.

4. To Kavita – a poetry of life

Do you remember that day?
perhaps yes, but you would not agree
but, I remember it today as vivid as that day
when you came into my dry world
to add a dimension to my pointless life
a point got stretched into a line and a line into a plane
to fill the volume of my inner vacuum.

I felt it in all my veins, the pressure of blood in my heart
sending waves to my mind and whirls to my thoughts
creating a feeling of new freedom and experience
of your very presence with charming smile, articulation
and graceful behavior, tenderness and rhythm of poetry.

My soul got elevated and ego inflated
my mind, thoughts flew high to skies and beyond oceans
still roaming in your thoughts every moment of wakefulness
months and years rolled - swept by the nasty wings of time
for the time never waits for anybody.
The circles around the eyes became darker and annular
the hairs turned grey, white
the face bore the wrinkles and indents
engraved by the onslaught of constant and perpetual rambling
in your cherished memories at times sweet and at times bitter
for there was yet no hope of reconciliation.

Like a baby it - my mind - clung to you
where ever you went to your own commitments or
to attend other longing souls like me
and it will not learn to forget you
the uncompromising and reserved as you seem to be
in all humility I must say.

Bewildered I ask him, -it, -my mind, -me, straight
how long, how far will you go?
but it has no answers and no questions either
and it continues to go on like rivers
flowing from Himalayas to plains
in ceaseless search for the redemption
into the vastness of fathomless ocean.
Not knowing the answers
the mind like a baby lies in your astral lap
to feel the warmth of your quantumness
and affection from your heart
looking deep in your eyes for guidance and care
for your graceful look to sooth itself.

Beyond the Earth you are like a horizon
which is never reached on an approach
in the plains - you are like a mirage
which is there but never there - an illusion
you are far, far away but the presence is spontaneous
on the stage of my mind's consciousness where
the play of varied thoughts is enacted.

Yet you are not within any sensible reach
distanced by the invisible walls and barriers
erected by my own limitations, ego and the fear of the world
that continues to be in a constant flux of change
and the horizon alluring my mind
with the harmless, unadulterated moments spent with you.
The sun rises from and sets into the horizon
the tides rise from and recede into the deadly vast ocean
the dreams come and fade away
leaving behind the fragrance and sweetness
of lively presence of someone like you who
continues to visit constantly the old house of my soul and
mind.

Making me feel good that there is
someone so benign like a petal of rose
that there is someone whose memory
brings a kind of tranquility to my mind
that there is someone who is unreachable
and yet enriches the soul that is ever in search of love and care.

That someone is you
but you will not agree
but I feel it that way
even today as vivid as that day
when you journeyed into the realm of my empty soul
and my confused mind to make me write about you and (to)
you.

5. Parental family

My Mother

Embodiment of the almighty Nature
full of love, affection and endurance
with unbelievable compassion and resilience unsurpassed.

Nourishing, nurturing her children
constantly caring for their health
needs and pleasures with utmost care and sentimental
affection.

The human Goddess of the Universe
more natural than one can imagine
with no trace of ego or arrogance
in supreme command of her wealth of love.

Yet fragile and weak
with imprints of bygone hard times on her face
approaching the old age rapidly
on the path to convolve into her own mother-Nature.

My Father

Soul only one of his kind
with finite powers and means
but with a strong mind, unceasing activity
with fountains of energy.

With limited knowledge but unlimited will
sailing through hostile environment
traveling and rallying for reforming the society
yet never tiring or retiring from the crusade.

Inspiring and caring soul
God fearing, loving
full of sacrifices and sufferings
yet never complaining or grumbling.

As if born to live for others
years full of work and ideals
died poor as he was
the soul that he was - the leader of rich life.

Death of the mother - My other mother Motali's world

I wrote poems Birth of a mother and
Growth of a mother but
had no courage to write one on death of the mother for
I do not want any mother to die ever
but, the death of all biological objects and species is inevitable
- the death remaining a reality
being an inevitable blow to human's confidence.

Finally I bowed down to this fact of life and
penned a poem for my Motali who was small and
fragile and displayed a deceptive smile on her face
tender in nature and simple in her demands
was fair and of thin frame
still highly likeable - especially to me for
she gave me whatever I wanted.

His was a shared world between Motali and my mother
always very busy with his professional work
or social activities — that were too many
but he, perhaps, liked it only that way
was already married once before with some children
from his first wife, no body knows much about them.

Motali was simple and honest without
any pretensions of any kind
a bit reserved and singular
avoiding shows and publicity
knew well her work and demanded no favors.

Any thing I wanted she would give me
made special food items for me
served them to me with happiness
played with me showering lot of affection on me
taking care of my things and stuff
saying prayers to guard me off from all evils.

She came from a nearby village
was a daughter of the head of the village
she carried an aura of a 'small beauty queen'
unfortunately had created an impression of
being lazy and not functioning
her fragility became prone to diseases
started falling sick quite often.

Being routinely treated by medicines and injections
as if administered to her skeleton
still mentally very strong and stubborn
would not easily give up
in later days of her life
remained sick for much longer time
and was bed-ridden.

One afternoon she gave up
I was summoned to 'yell' in her ear
"O my mother"!
for her own son was away
I yelled 'O my mother' into her ears
making bonds for eternity.

Sister

As innocent as a child you were
when we used to play and eat together
in the days of youth and joy
be it a cold winter or hot sun.

The years rolled by
the moment of separation came
to bid farewell to the nearest and dearest ones
to get on with the life of your new home.

The imprints of toil and hard work
peeping through your eyes
making you feeble, fragile
with no sign of remorse on your face.

The life full of sacrifices, endurances
for the healthy integrity of the other home
that became your own dutiful passion
bearing the burden almost single handed.

Child

Is the father of man
a little father of humanity
innocent and benign
bubbling with joyful energy.

Going through the pangs of life
already at this tender age
with diseases, vaccinations
fevers and coughs.

Learning to speak and walk
falling to rise again
treading long paths towards the successful growth
for fulfillment of the aim of life.

The joyful years of rolling on the dusty floor
running in the pools of muddy waters with freedom
the warmth of love and care from every one
all this freedom is going to be curtailed soon
when you enter the adulthood.

6. Wife

The half soul of a man
other wheel of Samsar chakra- worldly cycle
but carrying the full burden of life
and its routines and conventions.

Nursing and caring the husband
concerned of his health, his relatives and friends
yet unconcerned of her own problems.

More than a friend to her husband
more than a companion, more than many others things
yet at the husband's commanding services.

the life would have been dry without her
the home would be just a burrow sans warmth
the living would be burdensome
the fascinating and enduring soul-partner
who shares the pleasures and pangs of life
yet how much do we care for her?

7. All alone

In a place oceans away
landing there one day
in a camp of unknown land
new places and people
being in a room all alone
feeling terribly lone all alone
with no one to talk and meet
everything looking so different and new.

Memories of the past flood the mind
the heart full of emotions and
cherished memories of affection and love of loved ones
bringing out tears unceasingly
with loneliness all alone hoping to be short lived
in a place oceans away.

8. Work is worship

Work is worship – they say
it keeps us engaged and active
keeps us away from grumbling
gives company every where.

It is full of routines and chores
repetitive and at times boring
yet mandatory to maintain the life line
like heart and brain working for the life time.

The tiny ants, bees working
for food and procreation
for themselves and for others too
work seems remedy of many ills.

A great companion to man
relieving him of his loneliness
disciplining the mind and body
with sense of happiness and fulfillment.

9. Layer by layer

Pain expands from one layer
into the other layer
feeling it layer by layer and not as a whole at a time.

Mind expands from outer layer
into the inner self
experiencing its shades in stages and not in entirety.

Feelings evolve in stages
into inner soul
we experience them in quanta and not in abundance at a time.

Understanding expands in strata
into the cell of wisdom
we experience it in facets and not in it fullness at a time.

Wisdom is gained in stages
from inner intellect realizing in bundles of joy
hoping to expand to a total blissful state.

10. Your mere presence

You came and did not even talk - just went away
without even whispering a single word into my ear
but your mere presence left an aura of a kind.

It created an ambience of tranquility and serenity
silky touch of unselfish care and affection
without even touching me physically
your mere presence inspired and enlightened me.

Your bright eyes with benign smile on your face
just conveyed your sagacity
without even expecting anything in reciprocation
your mere presence created waves of happiness in my existence.

Your gestures and personality
subtle ways of communing to my mind
without even showing any sign of obligation
your mere presence trickled my inner soul with joy.

11. Timeless space

Space is finite in our rooms and hearts
infinite in nature and outwardly
the narrow minds and souls imprison it
to aggrandize and possess.

To divide it in cells is a modern day civilization
to control for petty gains and selfishness
to grab from weak to become rich
that is called cultured and sophisticated!

That all pervading space
timeless, boundless
never pulsating, yet supporting the evolution
window to the nature of the Almighty.

Rolling into itself but never contracting
mystery of science and philosophy
nurturing and enduring the humanity
beyond the grasp and destruction by humans.

12. Space-less time

There is a definite time as we see it
but it is timeless too
it is dynamic too
for it never waits for us.

It is static
for it is not seen moving
only there is 'tick tick' in a clock
chasing us all the time.

There is always a time for everything
but at times it is not there at all for us
if we do not cash on it
it runs out of our hands.

That is the time
with its space-less and timing characteristics
who can divine what is in the womb of time!

13. Time just stops

The time just stopped to see them together
in a close companionship to see how they talk, live together.

It really halted against its own nature
to feel the warmth emanating from their courtship
in a total union to see how they make love, rejoice.

The time actually became steady to see their playful movements
in a complete engulfment to see how they got engaged in the
act.

It surprisingly did not move at all
to fully register their enjoyment, satisfaction
in absolute fulfillment to see
how they comply with the natural force.

The time finally decided to move ahead
to be on its own normal dutiful journey
in exact agreement with its own nature
to see many more wonderful phenomena of life.

14. Existence

You call it Universe or Cosmos - call yourself 'Tony' or
'Radhika'
both belong to the Cosmos under Cosmic Laws
without which their existence is purposeless
both evolve in harmony adding rhythm and beauty
in confluence with space and time
to the dancing Cosmic existence
yet we are lost in our dreams and thoughts
in our actions and engagements
are lost in outer selves without any understanding
of the self and its universal existence.

Pure reign is religion, pure nature is religion that is existence -
like vast ocean behind the waves
the Atman - the being (-true self)
not the becoming is the existence.

We see the outer world in the wakeful state, dreams in sleeps,
only can we feel the self by the power of intuition
in the meditative confluence with the existence.

15. Indian river

Your flowing waters are chill and vibrant
often you are calm and warm
occasionally diverting to other pastures and creating new
paths even though shallow surrounded by green jungles
flocking your serene and serpentine anatomy
and yet your depth is unfathomable.
Treading long routes to meet your destiny – the ocean
en route providing succor to millions
occasionally showering your temper on those
who underestimate your prowess and fury.
Most take a dip in your waters and feel redeemed of their sins
others watch your flowing beauty from the banks
and feel gratified and elevated in their spirits.
A few - like me - wait far away from you scared of your chills
and temperament.
Hoping to approach you when the tides are over and to plunge
in your waters to 'drown' in the eternity that you are.

16. In a village

In a village at the bank of the river
running and playing the games
falling in the chill waters of the 'Himalayas'
only to be rescued by the fellow boys.

Swimming was unknown as were also the valleys
and the surrounding jungles with stormy winds
the roarings and cries of the wild animals
and the frightening cold and dark nights.

Soothing hospitality of the villagers
known to be poorer of the poorest
inscribed onto their faces
imprints from hard work, toiling and boiling in hot Sun.

And yet full of love and affection
beaming from their rusty and dusty faces
from their manners and gestures
making permanent bonds of eternity.

17. Friendship

The memories of the past association
spring up on the plane of mind
in the trance of sweet experiences
reliving the happiness
joy of the past years.

Though far away is near you
for there is nothing like far away
the space and time shrink in true friendship
with spontaneous love.

Come cyclones and rains
to slacken or weaken them
the bonds are so strong and evergreen
the distance is of no consequence here.

18. You are just wonderful

You are really wonderful
so many virtues
so many abilities
effortlessly dealing with
so many problems, people daily
tirelessly engaging in
numerous tasks and
joyfully completing them
devoid of any desire and selfish demands.

You stride by leaps and bounds
your presence simply brings
serenity with calmness
wonderment with peace in the vicinity
your resilience with sagacity creates
an atmosphere of oneness
an aura of inspiring self confidence.

19. Floods

She looked much tired but her wrinkled face
conveyed all the pain, loss and the sorrow
the people had suffered due to the devastating floods
yet at 99 Maya Devi full of optimism and zeal
yelled 'Jai Mata ki, Jai Bharat'.

Undeterred, undefeated she recounted the event-
'the swirling and gushing waters woke me
more and more water came pounding
my people pushed me onto the roof
the house was washed away
the Faujis – the soldiers rescued many of us'.

The river turned into the unbroken sheet of water
breaching bridges and Bandhs (-dams) and carrying away
some relief workers into the far other side of the country.

The media and politicians surveyed the area
only to see the floods receding away.

20. Nature's fury

Nature's fury - unpredictable, untimely, devastating
undermining the pride of human existence
and the technological progress
with phenomenal, formidable, dark and colossal powers
working on the scales of un surmountable distances and forces.

It seems uncertainty rules the roost
rush to catch it and it slips of your grasp
you think you caught it and it laughs at you
often you feel you remained where you were or are.

But it still gives us a chance to
fight back, improve, think and even wonder
gives us jolts in life beaconing to new avenues and hopes
leads us through the cycles of evolution
always reminding us it is only one and the most powerful.

21. War kills more than just soldiers

Wars over the eras killed millions of soldiers
thousands of innocent human beings
it destroys other lives too
animal kingdom, vegetation and what not!

Kills one's morale, motivation
destroying pride, chastity of women
disrupting the economical balance of
the nations at war
depleting the resources.

Leaving behind all people with humiliation
unbearable agonies, miseries and
false pride of the winner
over the ashes of humanity.

22. Fighting

I read epics Mahabharata, Ramayana
and find stories of fightings
between cousins, Ramas, Ravanas.

Then I wander into the lanes of the history of the world
see wars between kings
for women, wealth and fame.

When I stride on the streets of the modern rich world
I find urchins racing, fighting in the lanes
for rags and food.

I sip tea with the morning news of fightings
between saints, sheers - the learned men, women of wisdom
for temples and monuments.

I see the evil working in even
the minds of those who also pray God
tragically and unfortunately their priorities misplaced.

I ponder on the misguided souls
find them loosing the true meaning of life
that can be so beautiful and heavenly
for everyone on this Earth.

At the end may we pray for the lost lives
that were bubbling with zeal and innocence
and for those who sacrificed their loved ones.

23. Ruins of the world

Here powerful kings and deadly warriors fought
for dynasties, kingdoms and for women, princesses,
for wealth, pride and built the castles, towns, cities, empires
and the tanks, temples and mosques.

Many generations, civilizations and cultures rolled and swept
by swift and heavy tail of the cruel time
"that destructive power of the humans' wicked minds" only
could leave the cries and sufferings of many and
the skeletons and skeletons, baby-skeletons within bigger ones
buried in the ashes and ruins underneath
for one to dig out the wonder-tales and awesome stories
from the strained corridors, from broken gates of the prisons
and the death stones of the deadly executioners
from the obnoxiously smelling gas chambers
and the lanes of the ancient histories to resurrect the gory past
for its awesome glory? what glory? - dug by the archeologists
sung for centuries by the historians
whatever that may 'mean to a humble and weary traveler'.

24. Mid-air wish

You invaded our free territory
polluted our pure air-space with fumes, noise and sonic booms
frightening us while we fly peacefully
and soar under the heavens, breath Nature's air
we feed on leaves, seeds, flowers and a few insects
demanding nothing from the mankind.

You soar heights over seven oceans cutting the space-time
boundaries, hurting and hitting us - blaming us
for the damages to your giant flying machines
you spent years and precious money on research over the
'bird-hit' problem, forgetting a common - sense solution
'just steer clear away from our legitimate paths'!

You learnt from us and our kinds to fly, soar and flap the
wings
you bagged awards, prizes and fame from your peers
then used these instruments and technology
for waging and winning wars
over petty aims and egos
leaving behind millions of your own people dead and hungry
not sparing even me - your own teacher!

Baby - you have still not learnt
how really to fly like me!
even after hundred years
and millions of money spent.

It is my last dying wish
may you learn to fly with perfection and humility
for peace and prosperity
and for clean environment.

25. A steep fall

You told me to look at you and I did-
deep into your eyes and mind
I went around and above
the pebbles, rocks and mountains.

With a big thud I fell
into a deep, dark forest valley
still staring at you
for you had told me to do so.

26. Fire of desire

Its red hot fumes
originating from the valley of ignorance
move all around
to warm the body of a benign man.

Ignited more intensely by
the follies of human actions
entering the human mind
to leave it burnt out.

Creating the sensation in the soul
giving temporary pleasures
gushing hotter and hotter
to engulf the wisdom of the benign man.

27. Life machine

I see people rushing to jobs
by fast trains and buses or on bicycles
and still I see other people without jobs
waiting for screening tests and interviews.

Yet the life machine is on, embracing
all the people of the Earth in its groves
people going up and down in their lives
a few becoming rich and poor overnight.

The time is dynamic
and life is never static
those who comply enjoy real life and
the beauty of the nature - its cycles and seasons.

Others live painful machine-life
full of worries and vagaries
drudgery and boredom
waiting to perish in the mother nature.

28. Dreams

Dreams come and vanish
during bright days and dark nights
about people and places
murders and wars.

Seemingly real and vivid
but unreal and fragile
about our actions and deeds
our emotions and worries.
Resurrecting our past
relieving the tensions
about persons we love and hate
and events around us.
Expanding and contracting in our mind
flimsy, fascinating and often exciting
telling about our successes and failures
and unfulfilled ambitions.

29. Chaos

Look for it and it is there
in matter and mind
in clouds and winds
in the Universe and the Cosmos
and in mind's restlessness.

The soul often wandering in chaotic selfishness
that is chaos engulfing humans and their humanity

Will order emerge from the chaos?
it is for us to discover
a semblance of an order in the disorder.

30. Unity

Where is the unity?
is it there or here
in a village or a city
in a community or a country.

Is it really there? or is it just a mirage
alluring every one small or great
from all walks of life.

Is it really in our hearts?
or in our minds
or in our nature
or only in our speeches and gestures.

Where is the true unity?
that is so enigmatic
yet every one wants and waits
perhaps, it is here and here only
up to every individual to strive for it!

31. Yet one more ray of hope

In rains with torrential waters
muddy splashes and chilly winds
when I was caught up
you came in and opened up
your umbrella over me.

Although fully drenched
I felt good
and your act of helping me
kindled my soul
with a ray of hope.

In winter with cold winds
with chilly freezing nights
when I was shivering
you came in again and unfurled
your blanket to wrap me in.

Although almost frozen
I felt really good
and your act of caring for me
warmed my soul
with yet another ray of hope.

Tomorrow in summer with scorching heat
and burning winds
when I would be working in farms or streets
you will come again
with your umbrella.

Although almost burnt then
I will feel cool and good
and your act of caring for me
will enlighten my soul
with yet one more ray of hope.

32. Illusion of matter

The matter is as a 'matter' of fact not only matter
it is hollow at the microscopic level
with protons, electrons and neutrons, many more particles
of infinitesimally small dimensions
with lot of vacuum-space within.

Apparently the human body is matter, mind, intellect
looking and feeling solid and yet full of water-matter
water full of gases-hydrogen and oxygen
mind full of thoughts-good and bad
intellect beyond comprehension
where is then the solidity?

Everything that is solid is hollow, everything hollow is empty
emptiness having infinite space
space within space pointing to vast expansion
baffling, beyond the comprehension of the intelligence
yet existence seems 'real' and filling the vacuum of space.

This is the illusion in life
the 'Maya' (illusion - concept) of the world-
that is there and here but no where
it is both real to senses but in reality non-existent
the entire world is caught in its magical spasm
feeling the pains and pangs of daily routine living
not being able to get rid of Maya's clutches.

33. Mirage

I see it on roads, on bright hot Sunny days
On sandy deserts and rush to fetch the water
I see it receding away, the thirst remaining unquenched.

I thought I grasped the situation, but I only got a flavor of it
I thought I touched a drop on a petal of the lotus
It just vanished in the pond.

A constant search of an identity gave me only a glimpse of it
where do I belong in these galaxies of the Cosmos?
I thought I am in a realm of the reality
but I only 'felt' a fragrance of it.

I longed a life time for true love, I only got a trace of it
tirelessly searching a purpose of the life and its mission
but sensed only a touch of their tentacles.

And we all became mirages for each other in search of the truth
in our evolving lives reverberating only in earthly existence.

34. A jet age saint

He is a philosopher professing religion
overnight turned into a saint
with many names and ashrams
Mercedes cars, foreign devotees
with a field of saffron clad seekers of the truth
he is richer than the richest.

Gaining freedom from the chores of worldly life
responsibilities, routines of the busy life otherwise
searching real truth that yet
nobody knows where it is and what it is
and the Master is yet
not free from the follies of a normal human
a flying and globe trotting modern day saint
dies a death of a mortal.

35. Shiva's cosmic dance

I am Shiva – borne out of Hindu mythology
yet not created or really borne
I existed then, now and for ever will I exist
not created by anyone
yet presumed to be the creator of the universe-the cosmos.

I reside in your mind - am your mind itself
am your thoughts too
I reside in your body - still have no boundaries.

I dance in your mind as your thoughts
make you dance to the tunes of the pulsating life
that I have created or evolved !
for me to live for ever and ever.

You think you are living all the odds
and carry the burden for entire life
not realizing they are
my musings and doings.
I dance everywhere and every time
creating the waves of energy
that give you a meaning to your life
and you think you are defining
your life and its purpose.

My dance creates whirls and vibrations
more and more I dance
it creates more and more lives
more and more rhythm in the cosmos
I pervade everywhere and every time.

I am the ruffle of leaves in the trees
am eruptions of volcanoes, tornadoes
flowing waters in rivers, am thunderstorms and lightening.

I am silence too in your mind
intellect in your judgment
my dancing steps are throbs of your heart
creating feeling of love in you
for you to transcendent to me.
I am sound in the strings - am your magical voice
am roar of a lion
and far cry of a dying soul
and silence and vacuum thereafter.

I am fragrance in flowers
benign movement of a caterpillar
am the rainbow in the sky and colors of butterflies
am vast oceans and blue waters and the fang of a snake.

I create and destroy as well
that is my nature
to always be innovative and perpetuating
for infinite time and in infinite space
for a constant presence and eternity.

That is my cosmic dance
giving nectar of life to everyone
to every living creature and organism
am eternity-principle in all the objects of the universe
I am the Shiva-your cosmic dancer.

36. Wheel of selfish genes and spirituality

We are made of genes-they perpetuate for millions and millions
of years by shear force of their selfishness to exist
when we are borne we do not know we are selfish
we rejoice birth of a new baby innocently
we had waited for months to see it and we all begin to grow.
On the path of our growth we study various aspects of life
around us we study people, places and events
religious philosophies of the world
practice religions either ritualistically or philosophically
do prayers and visit places of worship
acquiring knowledge of science and spirituality.

Practice yoga, austerity and at times chastity,
these we do by our choice or the conventions set in our
community or society, often influenced by
the teachings of the religious masters of the past ages.

A few of us display high level of spirituality
and many show emotional intelligence or cognitive intelligence.

The masters have propounded this lineage
of the higher and higher kind of knowledge
by years and years of selfless studies
by analysis, thinking and experiences during their lives
either penned all that down or communicated orally
from generations to generations
making it profound, authentic and sacred knowledge
periodically getting further refined and modified
due to continual quest by
the evolving minds in the search of the absolute Truth.

The studies originating from our natural quest to search
search anything that we want, we desire or aspire
observing the natural phenomena taking place around us
and wondering how they happened and
our thinking machine sets in motion.

We speculate, calculate, imagine, and analyze these events
in the process getting some enlightenment
small incremental understanding, and the process grows
much of the knowledge of science and its enquiry
falling in the category of the cognitive intelligence.

What is very close to the 'spirit' of the self or existence
is the 'intellect' - being considered at higher level
much more profound and everlasting
than conventional intelligence
with much more Universal appeal
dwelling in the domain of spirituality.

We get scared of darkness, thunderstorms and wild animals
and we invent the concept of the so-called "GOD"
to mitigate our fears, uncertainties, and unknowns
we feel S/He will save us from calamities and death
attribute all good happenings to him/her
and live on hopes.

We have invented by such studies for thousands of years
the highest kind of spiritual tenets for us
and for our fellow beings to follow
the most sophisticated and highly refined kind of "selfishness"
so that, if our children and brethrens follow and practice them
they can live happily without much fear and uncertainty.

So that they can remain protected and
perpetuate their off springs
we strongly believe that following good path of actions
by doing good to others and helping others
we will earn the punyas-positive favors from God
to get rid of the sins committed knowingly or unknowingly.

Our goal is just to be happy
to prosper and attain fame
and be remembered for ever
and there is nothing wrong in it
if founded on the principle of live and let live
with exceptional aberrations.

On the path of our professional and personal development
we encounter the concept or theory of "selfish genes"
that propel themselves for the prolonged existence
for millions and millions of years
they do not seem to exhibit any purpose

being selfish at the fundamental core micro-level.

How they mould an individual to be highly spiritual?
selfishness being an antithesis of spirituality
does the "training" of thousands and thousands of years
render them to be "unselfish", at macro level,
to show nice and altruistic behavior
compatible with the tenets of spirituality?

As the life continues to evolve from mundane and
basal behavior to the higher kind
do these genes adapt to the new requirement of spirituality?
by compromising or cooperating rather than opposing
and still continuing to survive with "fundamental selfish"
behavior? - can we call them selfish, compromising and
cooperative genes simultaneously?
Selfish genes and the spirituality –
the 'dual' nature of our existence
the two sides of the coin-of-existence
one cannot exist without the other
spirituality is propelled by the existence of the selfish genes
the highest cannot exist without the lowest
the lowest has no purpose of existence without the highest.

Both co-exist may be at different scales of evolution of the self
the significance of the lowest, the concept of the "selfish genes"
evolves from the study by the highest brains
by the thinking minds, by highly evolved minds
and highly evolved studies of the nature
its evolution and its implications on human lives.

The existence of the selfish genes
and the existence of the spirituality
seem dual nature of our own existence
one depending on the other
one cannot sustain without the other
one having no purpose to exist without the other.
Co-existing in unison
they revolve around each other
getting strengthened by each other's evolution and development
yet maintaining their fundamental nature
and the most powerful presence
the greatest wonderment of the life and its nature.

Life itself seemingly a very complex process
spreading its tentacles to infinity
far beyond comprehension
the question of existence of life being universal
it exists, but why it exists
is less understood.

Acceptance of the concept of duality of existence of life
could parallel our acceptance of the duality
of the co-existence of quantum-mechanical
and wave nature of the matter
at the microscopic level
as we understand it today.

Spirituality evolving from the selfish genes - via our intellect
the genes - very 'us' at the core level
the genes have the purpose to evolve us
to the highest level
the level of spirituality ? – the experience of the blissful joy
one evolves from the other or
one has a purpose to evolve the other!
both work in unison without our
explicit awareness and knowledge
providing the rhythm of life in our lives.

37. Now you are old

Once you were young and energetic
full of strength and vigor
dynamism and activities
productive, persisting and aggressive.

You were youthful and racing
full of emotions and ideas
ideals and actions
consistent, compassionate and caring.

Now you are old
full of problems and complaints
living in past memories of your deeds
feeling utterly weak and powerless.

Having grown old and feeble
you feel an inward emptiness
and are helpless to withstand
the inevitable onslaughts of time.

38. Death

Death is deadly, devastating
sparing no one
rich or poor, young or old
man or woman, king or slave.

It comes silently or suddenly
casting sorrow and loneliness
making one wail and weep
creating the feeling of dejection.

It redeems the soul
to heavenly abode
before the dead is even cremated
buried or exposed to birds.

Death is here to come and stay
to transform the living beings
from old life to newer ones
with its deadly silence

39. Rebirth

On the mosaic of my mind
a thought flashed - Who am I?
where did I come from?

Bewildered I plunged for an answer
into the volumes of Vedas, Upnishads, Geeta and Puranas
and met Pundits and Seers.

I thought of Krishna, Rama, Jesus and Prophets
of great Saints - men and women of wisdom
heroes of histories of the world.

Still with confused mind
I - my mind - dashed into the heaven of Gods and Goddesses
in quest of an answer that my mind sought
and confronted with the Lord of Heavens.

The angered Lord due to my ignorance
and my futile search for thousands of years
wrapped me up in the layers of Heavenly mud
and paste of flowers.

And gave me a soft heavenly roll out - push
and I landed in my mother's womb again
where I sucked her 'food' for my nourishment.

I grew into a full baby - human in nine months
kicking on the inner walls of her womb
in an apparent rebuttal to Lord's punishment to me
and impatient to roll out of my mother's womb.

Into my own self once again in the intriguing outer world of
pains, pleasures, chaos, confusion
with discordant noises and hasty life
finally I was born with those
gift wrappers - from the Lord of heavens
but stinking and nauseating due to the earthen molding
yet with un-heavenly answer to my mind's quest!

40. Resurrection

You rushed unconcerned of the
presence of others, yelled at me
pulling me out of the bus
in a greater hurry and dragged me on the road.

Along with your friends
poured petrol on me to light me into fire
which burnt me completely
my soul left on the path to unknown.

You all gathered there to see
me burning to rejoice
the ugly and un-pious act of yours
others helplessly watching the scene.

You burnt me as if
you would burn a paper or piece of wood
my life had no meaning to you
your living is no honor to human society.

You dragged me in the kitchen
and poured kerosene on me and lighted the match stick
to burn and remove me from your life
then told I got burnt due to fire from the stove.

You caught me in a huff with lewd cunning eyes on me
torn my garments and floored me
to make me ready for your evil desire and forcibly
destroyed my purity and chastity.

They jailed and released you on bail
with lots of money spent
you all got scot-free from the ghastly
crime that you had committed so effortlessly and willfully.

You did that, for I did not belong to your religion
your kind or thought-line and was too feeble
or I did not bring lots of money and dowry for you and your
family- your mother, sister, even your own daughter
all my kind and my kind only!

41. Beginning the end…ending the beginning…

Every beginning has its end
and end ushers into a new beginning of another type
we move in blocks of time and space, often forward
at times and more often, more so backwards
yet continuing to make new beginnings
realizing sorrows, pains of our actions

one's pleasure and happiness are sorrows of someone else
no gain without loss of something or sacrifice
the nature forcing a balance between the two
the cycle goes on
either with existence or not, of the living beings

dynamic action being the characteristics of the nature
wherein everything that begins ends, the ends expand
into new era and endings begin again
we all try to live with living, cry with crying
die with the dying…beginning the end…
ending the beginning…

42. Her space

Her pre-space is orange, white, green
she is orange - dynamic, evolving, rising, fire-hot and bubbling
with energy
she is white — pure, calm, chaste, serene
she is green — the life provider, cool, wet
she is all in one and one in all.

She is mother, sister, wife, daughter, even a grand daughter
she is multi-dimensional, multi-faceted
she resides in us, out of us
strides from planet to planet and encompasses the universe
her sub-space is the projection of the
Cosmos on this physical world.

Where in we all live together
we believe we live together, but we are far spread and live on
separated islands of our minds, we live separately but still we
know that we live in the same world
in her space and her embrace — the mother Nature.

43. Twins apart

Lovely children of beauty
tiny, tender and slender
full of life and excitement
transforming the house into a real home.

Laughter, cries fill the space
affection, love fill the hearts
care and nursing take away the boredom
coaxing and persuading take away the time.

Kept separate to reduce chores at home
to lessen the burden on the mother
her heart torn apart with twins apart
as if splitting the affection and love to the twins apart!

44. Growth of a mother

Experiencing full joy and excitement
feeling the sense of fulfillment on
achieving a proud status of the mother
she is borne with the birth of her first child.

She grows with the growth of the child
the child growing in the lap and hands of the mother
under her care and affectionate love
the child being the embodiment of the mother
she being the manifestation of the mother-nature
the nature being its own creation beyond creation
the mother grows in her stature and dignity
in the world of her own child carrying the message of the
mother-nature.

The child and mother coexist sharing love
and joy from each other
with the mother growing in the warmth and spirit of this joy.

45. People

The lights are off, the doors are shut
the thoughts are on - the people are fast asleep.

The dreams are lively, enchanting
incomplete and vanishing
then the people are awake.

The Sun is full bright, shining
the trains moving fast - the people hurrying to their jobs.

Shrilling noises of machines, train engines
with poisonous gases around - yet the people moving all
around.

The Sun is very hot, burning winds
the water is scare - yet people are traveling all around.

The crowding is too much
the stampedes occur
and yet people gather from far places.

46. Where and what is God?

Perhaps,
S/he is in our breath
in our mind and thoughts
in our actions.

Is the tenderness of leaves
is the colors of flowers and butterflies
in the instincts of animals.

He is the intrinsic intellect in us
in the force of our emotions
in the play of a child.

Is the texture of leaves
is colorful panorama of birds
in the spontaneity of thunderstorms.

He is the wisdom in us
in the force of our affections
in the love of the mother.

Is the pattern of the seasons
is colorful mosaic of sea animals
in the symmetry of objects.

He is the innocence of a child
in the lullaby of the mother
in the purity of the soul.

Is the space-time mystery
is colorful spectrum of the rainbow
in the regularity of the planetary motions.

He is the goodness in humans
in the force of love
in the creative and adaptive Nature.

47. Sweet warm home

I went to his house
it was in a small village
he was working for my father to help in his office work.

They fed me well and took me around in the streets
introduced to his friends and relatives
"This is my boss's son".

His mother spread a bed for me on the floor of the house
it was a very small old house
with flimsy roof as the shade.

The lights went off
got a first dose of sleep instantly because of heavy meal
but after a while things changed.

Bed bugs started working for their meal sucking blood of mine
others slept deep
all used to this daily menace.

Suddenly the rains started
the water started dripping from the roof
through the holes unplugged
I got up and started shifting my bed.

After a few shifts got to a safer spot
and slept well
feeling the sweet smell of the monsoon
all pervading and cooling.

Got up into the wet morning
a few streaking rays from the rising Sun
good morning, good morning
they asked if I had a good sleep.

Sweet hot break fasts
sweet pleasantries, good bye, thanks for coming
hope you did not have any problem
please come again to our home.

48. Journey

The train halted at the station
people rushed in and out of the bogies
unconcerned of each other-either way
unconcerned of sick and old.

Bus is cancelled, the trains are late
the taxis are costly, the rickshaws are full
pedals are prohibited
still people travel and move uncontrollably.

People are dynamic for attending
their jobs, visiting sick in hospitals, the religious rituals
for social reasons, personal matters, for settling claims
paying the bills, attending schools.

Facing delays, traffic jams, heat
the active and bold move all over
braving rains and accidents
the lazy and timid remain static where they are.
A half-naked begging boy sweeps the floor of the compartment
asks for something
you offer a piece or chunk of the food you are eating
he smells it and throws away there only.

You feel insulted and wonder why he behaved thus
what an ego while he is so hungry, that too being a beggar
you feel jolted, try to curse him less realizing that
that ego or an act of show-off, or display of superiority
is his only pride for his survival.

For he does not know who or where are his parents
over beaten by harsh realities of the begging life
does not have any shelter except
a footpath or corner of the railway platform.

Has not taken bath for weeks and the face
is black with soot and he is a skeleton in full
decades after the Independence
the poverty is still not gotten rid of
for millions are still under fed like him.
The train halts at the next station
the in flux-out flux of passengers repeats
with the same jostling
coolies yelling for carrying luggage and running fast
the passengers yelling on their mobiles.

Some rushing to the bus stations, taxi stands
some to airport or their cars
with the hectic life that does not like to halt
the train again moves whistling
with begging sounds and esteemed passengers!

49. Magnificent force and its awesome act

The stars are twinkling
the moon is rising
night is cool and calm
but her emotions are not
she is laden with lots of gold and silver
exotic garments and perfumes
mind full of thoughts of waiting moments.

Imaginations are at their art work
the heart is throbbing faster and faster
he will come any moment
blood rushing to the face red hot
why there is so much delay
I waited for so many years
and still how much more have I to wait.

A thought came and engrossed her
fully as if he himself came and embraced her
he will uncover my face and look deep in my eyes
he will be excited to talk to me
touch and feel me
smell my perfumes and feel my throbbing
feel my emotions and try to uncover me.

I will resist that move, I am shy type
but if insisted I will like that way only
the long awaited moment will come and he will get
engrossed in me and me only
would like him to move in my deeper realm
and my treasured world so far unexplored
for his total discovery of the new vistas.

A knock is heard at the door and he
really enters the fully decorated room
her thought is broken and the anxiety returns
approaching her, he is totally astonished
uncovering her face and seeing her splendid beauty
he is nonplus and his mind full of emotions and imaginations
shall I talk to her and ask her about her younger days?

Or wait for her to initiate the move
be it a whispering or winking of eye
or even closed eyes with a sweet smile on her face
whatever it be, it would be just great
superb experience of the life
the heavenly moment will approach
the moon will be calmer, the winds will stop.

His imaginations ran faster and faster
I will touch her smoothly and tenderly
and feel her warm breath and hot body
will go over pebbles and mountains
will explore her exotic beauty
the newer vistas of life and
fall into her dark black valleys with magnificent force.

While ramblings and tossing around I will
travel to uncontrolled, vast expanded avenues of herself
feeling the excitement every moment of
the voyage into the oceans of pleasures and happiness
never getting tired or bored, but
eventually getting exhausted with the
ultimate fulfillment of the divine flow and awesome act.

His thoughtful imagination broke when
she asked what kept you so late?
you made me wait so long and am feeling too sleepy
but very happy that ultimately you came
shall we talk over or go to bed?
they got entangled, engrossed and traversed into
uncontrolled fountains of colorful realities.

50. Agony love

30 years ago he came to a great city
for a job that fetched only 500 a month
and paid 150 as the rent for an outhouse
with a family of 3 he managed everything
in an unfamiliar street house that had
poor sanitation and crowded surroundings.

Worked very hard for everything to
achieve a good success and rise
gradually came up the ladder with
perseverance and sincerity
with zeal and enthusiasm
with courage and assertions.

The time has come now to retire
after years of service with
triumphs and tryst with unknown destiny
soon the ties will be broken up
the regular work will cease - the office routines will be gone.
Those were the days full of
challenges and excitement
at office and at home
newer and newer things to be
tried out and worked out
to maintain the rhythm at work and home.

Establishing the rapports with colleagues
with new people at office and in the neighborhoods
learning to grasp their moods and adjusting to
their working style and learning new language
making steady progress of work and working
relationships for the betterment of the self.

Now the things will be different
new relationships would be developed
new work or engagements would be needed
the age would have its effects
energies would be limited
yet the past would invoke the old memories.

Those were the years of commitments and fulfillments
growth and endurances
traveling to far away places beyond oceans and gathering
newer experiences and making new
bonds with places and people
professional and personal.

Making mistakes and learning from blunders
falling and rising again
making definite strides and progress
fulfilling the dreams and a few desires
gaining recognition from friends and peers
without any awards.

Soon things will change
the change being inevitable
the generations have rolled by
observing the change
bringing new vistas
new adjustments.

Those were the vibrant days
the days and years rolled by
leaving many imprints
some good and some harsh
on the minds of his family often
shaking him with unforeseen events.

The ordeals were a few but they left
definite scars and unpleasant tastes
as if undermining the achievements and honest living
shaking confidence occasionally
creating delusion and even illusions
spiraling to spin the individual.

Now the memories of the hard lives lived
would flood the mind and the thoughts
would flow in various directions in search of
some solace and guidance
from where?, he does not know
perhaps from newer knowledge, nobler attitudes.

In the later years it started going tough
tougher situations emerged
his family suffered setbacks for unknown reasons
not much to their faults
unpleasant situations and events arose
which could have been avoided.

It was perhaps a bad luck for the family
they were a soft family being
soft to others and respecting them
that was taken for granted as their
weakness or dumbness?
touching them very sensitively.

Even now the impressions are vivid
reconciling and interpreting the events
trying to forego and forget
the gory past agony experiences
of his beloved father's death
breaking of a love marriage in the family in a short time only.

Then they had a difficulty in accepting
such situations wherein the relations could become sour
they thought what is in the life to live for
if we do not live with care, with concerns
with affection for the loved ones
and enduring love?

With the grace of Almighty, with powerful prayers from
his devout and pious wife
with support and cooperation from the dear ones
with some inbuilt resilience in the family
with the births of their lovely "God"-sent
grand daughters they just-sort-of recovered from the shocks.

Now he would retire at 60, to be free for 365 days in a year?
with mixed feelings about people, places, events and
cherishing the memories
he thanked his colleagues and friends in the office
gave a short speech with chalked emotions
accepted a customary basket of fruits and flowers
then the driver came and said 'Sir, the car has come'.

51. I stopped the time again

Neither the scientists
nor the almighty Nature can stop the time
for it is awesomely dynamic
but, a poet can stop it!
and I did it once again
to show it the cruel phenomenon in the world
and the time stopped against its very dynamic nature
to watch a baby in the nearby dustbin!

Crying, abandoned by its "great" parents
who fearing the stigma
left their own tiny, tender, innocent and vulnerable
child to the care of the passers by, sweepers or dogs!

The time got upset with me and
curse the humanity at large
and in a swift anger slapped me and
dissolved into its own nature!

52. My reading of my poetry

My reading of my poetry reminds
me of my follies, the human follies
that my thoughts are infinite, but
I have only a few ideas
and the thoughts wonder in all directions
without any aim.

My reading of my poems reminds me
of my several limitations
my ego that limits my wisdom
where did my wisdom go?

My reading of my poetry
reminds me of my shortcomings
that are plentiful
I cannot fathom the depth of any true love
the anger runs faster than the thoughts
where from it comes and acts
I do not know.
My reading of my poetry tells
me of many pitfalls that
I have yet not surpassed
and I am far away from
redeeming my soul
from the bondages of this finite world.

53. The day of the judgment

The pin-drop silence in the courtroom
the silence that was never experienced
all the eyes and the minds on the judge's chair
that the judgment would be delivered soon.

She read out: the couple had tried hard to
be with each other
but now that they are not able to
after consideration of all relevant aspects
it is decreed that they are legally separated.

The silence and the deadly silence
now for ever in the lives of the two
that they wanted separation but
perhaps it was too early
that happened in their lives too suddenly.

They had not envisaged that
they will go this way
it was hardly two anniversaries
spent together in merriment
but they did not grasp the real
joy of being together.

They loved each other for several years
before they got married and the day came too soon
for the silence of the judgment
the separation and the loneliness
where did the affection and care vanish?
where did the true love disappear?

The life was then very hectic and busy
had no time for details and chores
the work was only the additional burden
pressure and demanding
there was no time left for reconciliation
and any fruitful discussions to sort out the matters.

The vagaries of the lives became
uncontrollable and taxing
the pills and counseling did not bring any succor
tensions grew and the performance dwindled
the wisdom did not prevail and the egos were hurt.

Finally the matters got sorted out
by the return of the silence
the silence of the judgment
the judgment for the silence
on the day of the judgment!

54. Stains on humanity

Some say we were sleeping for millions of years
the humanity has been sleeping for all these years!
I see myself on this planet rotating and revolving with it
and whirling around the giant Sun and with it further into
the vast galaxy and where not, I went in my un-wakeful state
and even in the wakeful consciousness, I would not know
into the formidable space for all these years!

I am scarred when I traveled so much and so far into
awesome Cosmos and I am still where I was earlier
pulled by the centre of gravity of the planet
keeping me steady and not being thrown away
so that I can breathe and live
breathe for what and live for whom?
to live I need oxygen and 'eat' cells
from plants and animals for energy
and my own survival
as such plants and animals are not waiting to be eaten
they do not know we are eating them and why
they do not know why they are here either
do we know why we are here?

We call ourselves as higher species than them
what higher, how higher, we are only because of them
for all their cells are 'cooking' in our stomachs
and working in our blood and 'thinking' in our brains
so that we can call ourselves more intelligent and brainy!
and we call ourselves higher species!

We kill animals for our selfish interests, for fur and ivory
we oppress and torture our own fellow humans
we cheat, loot them and kill them
burn them in gas chambers
or throw them in stinking prison cells for ever
and we call ourselves higher species!

We kill innocent people mercilessly and chillingly
in the name of the 'God', and I wonder
if the same 'God' approves this act of ours!
and I also wonder why He/She remains silent
on innocent people being killed by force and tyranny!

Though there is real abundance of foods on the planet
yet millions go hungry every day
live without medications and sanitations
for our decisions and rules are contrived
our religions offer heavens to them but they live in hell
deprived of privileges and rights
they live in mental blocks and bondages
without proper and adequate literacy.

We offer them promises and programs
spend millions of money on
technology developments and war machines
and we want to conquer the world
for whom and why and what for?
we do not really know - we are lost in illusion
we do not know where do we want to go
with all this progress when our own
kinds are still deprived of smiles
on their faces and real joy!

55. Musk deer

Oh! my 'God'
we seek 'GOD' in or through Jesus, Prophets and Heavens
some say the God is in your own heart
and we are circling like the musk-deer
searching the source of its own musk
not reaching there ever!

56. Fear of existence

Humanity and her humans are under a siege for centuries
they live under some existential pressures
being in race uncontrolled and uncensored
want to fly to higher altitudes, get rocketed into the far space
they want to conquer the lands, waters and space and the
globe
destroy the forests for more woods, oil and more plain land
in turn destroying the wild life
that is so natural and innocent on the Earth.

Humans are more 'selfish' than plants and animals which live
absolutely natural lives following
the rules of the nature - the evolution.

Humans' disturbed minds under the seizure of the existential
pressure - propels them to live contrived lives
not being able to understand and control the spasm of
uncertainties, unknowns, and unforeseen events and vagaries
of life - making unforgivable mistakes and blunders
under the seizure of the existential pressures.

57. The life is too short

The life is too short in this awesome
Cosmic wonder that is beyond the grasp of
even science, our minds and our intellects.

It might take billions of years for us
to fully understand all that
and by that time more
billion years of evolution would have taken place!

It is like a mirage - we thought we grasped it
and run to fetch water and it disappears.

During these few years on this planet
perhaps the immediate aim for the humans
is to live for each other in whatever possible way.

58. Dates

Our life is full of dates for exams and interviews
for weddings and appointments with doctors
for schedule of works and reviews
dates all over the calendars and internets.

All over the world now people go for dating
he will say, she is my date and she will say, he is my date
in the ultra modern world he says, he is my date
and she says, she is my date!

Wet and dry dates for eating, dates for business, transactions
for elections, the success of which is uncertain
the failed dates send us home worried and perturbed
and we curse someone or ourselves.

We have the dates with the nature
of which we are not worried or even count it
we do not bother about it ever!
we are dates-full dateless people any way!

59. A birdie

A bird sat on the yellow car
while I was approaching my car parked nearby.

It asked me, whose is this Yellow?
I said, it is my boss's car.

The birdie asked me, is he a big man?
I said, yes, very big, powerful and influential.

It said, then I won't spoil it
then it moved and sat on my car
and eased out itself fully onto the window!

I asked, why it spoilt my car.

It said, I know you for years
you were born in a village, on a cliff
and now you are 60 years old warned out guy
grew up in a town and somehow
educated in a city and got a job in a famous research lab

Then I said, so what?

It said to me
you think you are great but you are not
you still need to know more about us and the life
now you keep cleaning your car as my sweeper
by the way I liked it, it is a cute white Polo
I enjoyed easing out my droppings on it
and actually I was checking on your patience!
Dankie!

Then it said
ok-tata-bye-bye, anyway my
make-my-trip was successful
auf wiedersehen!

And the cute small colorful birdie flew away.

60. Life's 'prosy' Priorities

The first priority should be health
without which we cannot do any good job
good work for the office or even at home
cannot realize or fulfill our ambitions and dreams.

Then immediate priority should be job related matters
where from the money comes
to take care of our needs and health!
then immediate priority is the human
and public relationships
that keep us in good balance
indeed very useful in our emergencies.

The effective and affectionate bondages
enhance our confidence
in handling the outside matters and logistics
and also in our own self.

These aspects and engagements keep us
mentally, intellectually and socially alert and active
so that we can make progress in our lives
and meet our goals
which if lofty, inspiring and enlivening
will pave the way for our overall holistic
and long enduring development.

61. A few prosy odd people

It is unfortunate, but it is a fact
you would encounter a few 'odd' people
around you in your this short span of life.

They may not be so bad but
they still would bother you
grumble about you and would be
even jealous of your achievements.

They might be overly curious about your
activities, affairs and even personal life
they even would 'cook up' the affairs that
you never had and do not have either
may be it is in their nature to be so or do so.

They will have lot of misunderstanding
about you and your relationships with the people around you
they might define such definite relationships.

They might not intent to harm or hurt
but they might just do that
without being conscious of the
trouble created by them.

When confronted they will justify their actions
as just their curiosity, shear innocence and
no evil eye on your property or achievements.

If further questioned, they might feel offended
try to, as if, cut-off their relationship with you
and might keep quiet for sometime with no
hint that they might spring up again
with new ways and new reasons
as your watch dogs and to keep you on your toes!

To check on you, to keep you alert so that
you do not falter and deviate from your path
to your goals without they even knowing your goals!

62. Gift of evolution

Human life is full of surprises and uncertainties
this is the 'gift' of the evolution
you may call it a package from the 'God'
whether God exists or not, whether we believe in 'God' or not
we do exist.

Around us are several profound truths
different from the so called absolute truth
first we should try to understand and appreciate
these profound truths and their effects on our every day lives.

Then we should try to understand the illusions
these profound truths have created for ourselves
it is pity that many of us, and actually most of us
are not even aware of such aspects in our lives.

It is really amazing that our spiritual masters
-call them gurus, masters, spiritual leaders, rishis, philosophers
whatever – thousands of years ago
had said that the worldly-world is a myth.

How they came to realize this we really do not know
they at those times did not have much clue of
the evolution of the biological species
that we know it today better.

When I read books on spirituality and evolution
I feel ultimately these books are hinting the same things
in their own characteristic style.

In the entire cosmos, it seems there is no end goal!
whatever it is, it is the immediate goal
what an interesting confluence of
the thoughts from these great masters of the spiritual literature
and science literature!

We need to go yet several thousands miles
to understand all these
a path for us is to realize and feel these profound truths
their powerful illusions and the 'God'-hood of Love.

Our daily attempt should be to reduce the effect of these
illusions and uncertainties on our state of mind and being
and reach the real state of 'God'-hood of Love and
help others to raise their consciousness and enhance awareness.

63. Anny Good

I, from Bangalore, called her in Glasgow
and somebody told Anny is bed-ridden
how much I wanted to talk to her
and listen to her humble and lovely voice
but couldn't.

After a few days I called her again
and she picked up the receiver
she told me she is not well at all
and is bed-ridden and passed on the receiver to somebody.

Anny Good was quite old when I first met her
in her Glasgow house in September 1997
I had two dinners with her and her friends
all were devotees of Satya Sai Baba
of Andhra Pradesh and all were vegetarian.

She was even then very old and yet
vibrant, swiftly moving from the kitchen to the dining area
and offering varieties of food to her guests
I presented a small scarf as a gift to her and she
promptly displayed and wore it and told everybody
that she was very delighted to receive it – what a humble soul.

A very rich lady with such a humble nature
she served as a nurse and volunteer in several camps
of refugees and worn-torn people from warring countries
was quite short but very tall in her ideas and ideals
dressed in whites she looked like an angel
very committed, pious and 'God' fearing soul.

Sent to me greetings cards for several years
wrote nice messages and names of all my family members
and enquired of their welfare.

When the cards stopped, I got curious to know
and hence I called her only to know that
she was not able to continue conversation for long.
I do not know if she recognized my voice after several years
but I could hear her voice and
felt at least good that I could talk to her.

Anny Good - a service oriented human being and
the lover of humanity
a short lady with high dynamism yet
now quietly lying down on the bed.

I wish she is alright and lives yet longer
though she cannot do any work but
knowing that she is living, is really soothing
inspiring and a constant reminder that
hear is around us a 'God'-sent angel that is Anny Good.

64. Around the world – the worldly benedictions

We have gone through several trials and tribulations in
our lives and come a long way at this stage
we do feel reasonably satisfied and gratified.

All through got very good cooperation, care, affection and love
from all our children, relatives and friends
with some of them we have lost touch
due to distance or lack of enliven/active communication
from either or both the sides
-not with our own children luckily!

We have traveled lot in India and abroad, and we find that
the human needs all over the world
at micro level are the same: care, affection and love.

May you all, your own friends and relatives always
be in the state full of these
lovely and divine benedictions for your entire lives.

65. Creation?

Isn't it better to say that the things have evolved
the variety, the variations, the magnificence
all being awesome, awe-inspiring and
in the final analysis
all these might be or are pleasing and amusing to humans.

Isn't it more plausible and humble
to say that way rather than say
- the Nature has created all theses and made
to please the humans!

66. Shining

Due to the composition of the objects and people
in the empirical world (the Samsar)
their different trainings, dispositions, and interactions
we go through ups and downs in our lives
we go through several odds and ordeals and
face a few or more difficulties.

We need to endeavor to boldly face these odds
trials and tribulations to overcome all the hurdles
with determination, resilience, and courage.

These experiences making us more robust, more successful
more joyous and we shine in this world
much more than a reflecting mirror.

67. Worship

Worship (Puja) in real sense signifies
happening of completeness, creation of fullness
becoming of the full being.

By true worship one becomes a complete self
realizing oneness with the Universal truth
experiencing the becoming of the full being
the merging of the self-singleton into the 'Paramatma'.

68. True Prayer

Prayer is not the demand from the "God" –
give me this and give me that, do this and that for me, and
please do all these for me, O! my "God" please do!

True prayer is to feel thankful to the Nature
for what we have got
it being an expression of joy deep from within our hearts.

We see beautiful trees, colorful flowers, and panorama of birds
magnificent animals, and most fascinating colorful butterflies
all awe-inspiring in dimension and/or multitude
very long ranges of mountains, rivers, and several oceans
hugeness of planets and vastness of cosmos.

And our hearts inflate and we burst
with expression of shear joy, happiness and gratefulness
that is the true prayer to express, give and enjoy
and not demand or acquire.

69. God (Bhagavan)

God is the concept of sum total of
earth-the solidity, water, air, fire and sky.

He/she has to be resilient like the Earth – the solid
we dig it and it gives us gold, minerals
coal and crude oil and water
and it is still resilient and solid.

She/he should be like fire that can burn your ignorance
it is bright and shining and red hot
it can burn your follies and brighten you up.

He/she is like air, the minute and soft and un-catch-able
it signifies the sensation of touch, the feel and is life giver
the worldly happiness is felt by touch
only the infinitesimally small at the microscopic level
something like it can go through your heart and soul
the one who can go deep in your mind and touch you.

She/he is like water, the flowing, soft and naturally cool
the very basic need, and the life giver to entire humanity.

He/she is like space, the vastness and infinite
sustaining and encompassing everything in the Nature
the Cosmos, the Universe whatever you call it.

That is the God made of the basic five elements
with the qualities of
earth-the solidity, the water, the fire, the air and the space
the God-concept-the virtues to be imbibed by us the humans.

70. Glimpses of Gods of Hindus

There is 'light' in every being, that shines
that is consciousness that is called Rama.

Every living cell has to have energy and oxygen
and the energy can be created by destruction of mass
'with the speed of light'!
energy being equal
to mass times speed of light times speed of light!

The energy and oxygen together enliven the cells
energize them, brighten them and induce liveliness in them
the basic ingredients of the living beings
that one always shines in our hearts
that consciousness is called Rama.

That Krishna depicted as blue colored God
that is what is knowledge represented as blue color
the representative of infinite knowledge
the open sky is blue color - the vastness, the space
which is through and through, the endless space.

The Lord Shiva, the innocent, the lover and
yet the symbol of destruction!
creator of new things by destruction
and the great dancer.

Vishnu, the God who is cool and calm
full of ornaments, the maintainer of the world
the supporter of the world!

The Kali – the fear – inspiring!
the one with open mouth and displaying her tongue
with a sword in one hand, a (cut-out) head in the other hand
the blood dripping from the head
the head of a devil!
the necklace of the skulls around her neck!
if you can tolerate her, then you do not have fear
all problems start with our minds and
bad thoughts in our heads, the misunderstandings
the head symbolizing the problems
the cut-out head representing
the removal of the ego, the problems.

Saraswati, the Goddess of knowledge
cool, calm, serene, and peaceful
the knowledge inducing these tendencies and virtues in us
either worldly or spiritual knowledge, both very useful
in our daily lives, the latter propelling us to our redemption.

The Laksmi, the Godess of wealth
that is the need of everybody on this planet
for food, clothing and shelter
for the poor and even for the richer.

71. The body contact

Alas! we are mortal, but immortal, and yet mortal
we are both mortal and immortal simultaneously
and our mortal body seeks always a body contact
we like to chew things, break things, eat things
press things, and touch them and even crush some
without body contacts with the objects, people and places
we feel utterly left out, alien, ignored and isolated.

We accept inputs from our sense-organs and senses
touch, smell, taste, hearing, and visual and
even the sixth sense as mystics tell us
in different physical formats.

By some incredible process, not yet fully understood
in these organs and mainly in the brains, we transform
these inputs into the sensation of being in some "reality"
we need to feel or be assured that we are somewhere in
some coordinates, in some place at some time to obtain a
more complete picture of the observed world.

Much of our life depends on 'body' contacts good or bad
we need to touch and smell to see if something exists or not
children need hugs and kisses from parents and relatives.

The profound body contact is through sex
they say sex is a biological urge in humans
so is for many biological species, they not knowing it as an urge
either uni-or-bisexual, what ever it is
it is a tremendously powerful physiological force!
much powerful than the force of gravitation
and the nuclear forces in the matter, un-measurable it is!

It is a force of not only the physical magnitude and vigor
is also a force of the emotional intensity and
physiological process permanently present but
working on and off based on the needs and
at times not on any needs!
mainly realized, practiced only at the level of 'body' contacts
the multitude of components, of different sizes and shapes
hard and soft, muscular or not
working for its fulfillment, on and off, contracting and
expanding and yet always wanting to work as propelled by
the selfish genes to propagate themselves for ever and ever.

Sex is a misfiring (for humans) of the evolution
since the animals do when needed for procreation
for getting off-springs, the humans do for this reasons
even when otherwise not needed but
they do it for varieties of additional reasons
for showing off their power, for self-gratification
for building new relationships, for bonding ties
for showing masculinity and
for culmination of showing and expression of the love.

There is bad sex bringing agony, sadness, often leading to
unfortunate rapes, and varied criminality, abhorred by the
descent society and people at large, the sex misused and mis-sold
and there is good sex, bringing happiness, relaxation and
calmness, coolness and temporary peace.

The grip is such that due to its after effect, the world is
propagating for millions of years with new born
and more and more new born!

The most difficult to tame, calling for often heroic efforts to
regulate it even at a small scale
the enigma of the nature and its evolutionary game
the entire world seems to be caught in its spasm
with varied colors, meanings and implications
desired by one and many, considered as a gift of the "God".

72. Durban – Durban, agony affection

It is Durban and its beach area that are perhaps
the most magnificent, and the valley of thousand hills
and why not the hill of thousand valleys!
abundance of greenery, and cool Christmas winds and times

The picturesque place with colorful tourists, and multi-
cultural people, of different colors as some classify them as:
blacks, whites, even colored, and Indians, and others.

The history was different then, full of hatred and agonies, of
discrimination and continual struggle, wars and killings
now it is different with people freely moving and rejoicing in
merriment and excitement, and freedom at last gained through
struggle, heroic resistance, and assertion of ones rights to
peacefully and freely live in their own country of origin.

Beautiful cities with nice roads, and several wonderful natural
wild life game parks and tourist places, the Cape Town, Cape
point, Robben Island and well developed coastal areas
the lion safaris, and big fives, as they name these wild animals:
the buffalo, rhino, lion, elephant and cheetah in the Country.

The country of multitude of colors and religions and beliefs
with very rich resources, gold and platinum mines and
still the poor are poor, and under developed
still grasping with the misplaced realities and crimes
perpetrated by a certain class and color of people on their on
fellow beings and brethrens, unconcerned of the fact that these
brethrens and they themselves have to join hands together to
retain, maintain and nurture the democracy that they all have
so much struggled to regain, have sacrificed their kith and kin
and lost wealth, lands, health, and times which to again build
up will take hundreds of years of toil and labor.

73. A humble wish

I want to explore connections between Science, Evolution and
Indic philosophy-and may be other P'sophies of the world!
I have a humble desire to work on the theme
Infinitum: Profound truths, Powerful illusions and
'Godhood' of Love – A path to self realization
(or – A Poetry of Life).

There is the science of the Cosmos that we live in now
how much it might have not been understood
but some theories are prevalent, some practical proofs
and some analytical studies and investigations are here
for us to read, analyze and discuss and
if possible test them by ourselves.

Science has clarified many things for us
falling of an apple – an act of gravity
shapes and rotations of celestial objects, planets
understanding of diseases, working of kidneys and heart
eyes, ears, lungs and many more things.

Science has given us electricity and telecommunications
microphones, radios, cameras, TVs, computers and cell phones
artificial organs and gadgets
we can make bridges, dams and machines
and very costly technologies, even warring machines.

Where do the science, analysis and mathematics come from?
all these come from thinking brains
the brains are made of cells which are having the genes
the 'selfish' genes which propagate for millions of years!

Science and evolution are closely linked
— evolution is the science of living organisms
thinking brain of human is a confluence of
science, evolution and intrinsic intellect
which again is the outcome from the physical brain
which thinks many philosophies that guide us to the path of
righteousness, order, rhythm, harmony, and perfection
hinting at the confluence of science, evolution and
philosophies.

We should explore all these in further details and understand
the confluence of science, evolution and philosophies and
see if this can further enhance the
awareness and consciousness of our fellow humans.

That is the humble wish that
we all should hope and wish to fulfill.

74. Seek Almighty

"Seek Govinda, seek Govinda, seek Govinda – the Almighty, Oh
fool! When the appointed time comes – when you are approaching
the death - the grammar-rules surely will not save you" - SC (see the
notes/Glossary).

"Seek the Lord, seek the Lord, Seek, Seek, Seek the Lord,
Seek alone the Lord, the Lord...O mud-headed fool,
When the time to leave approaches you near,
You won't be saved by rules of Grammar"– BS (see the notes).

1. Oh! Fool

O! disciple, O! seeker, the seeker of the Truth
pack up your heart with the thoughts of the Almighty 'God'
sans excitement, sans anxieties, quit thoughts to acquire
to collect and posses secular achievements - the grammar rules.

When death approaches you, the time to leave this world
arrives,
the secular knowledge - the grammar rules
the routines and ritualistic practices are of no consequences.

When the death strikes its nail, and the deadly moment arrives
the science shrinks and the solidity disappears
the chemistry and reactions work to turn you into the ashes
which would fly all around, only the bones remaining to
fossilize and the soul (the Jiva) longing to be redeemed
into that peaceful and divine eternal existence.

Seek Almighty, the truth of the Cosmos, the 'cause'
of the Universe, and listen to and sing the glory of almighty
wonder the awesome nature and ponder over its beauty
that is the substratum of the world-play of the nature
that is the essence behind the living kingdom.

Their sounds, speeches, music and their musings
be it roaring of a lion, or chirping of a bird
be it an eloquent speech of a speaker
or the braying of an ass, the barking of a dog.

All and more the manifestations of the essential nature of the
existence—the Almighty nature, the essence of the Universe
that essence you seek, O! the estranged seeker!

"Oh fool! Give up the thirst to possess wealth. Create
in your mind, devoid of passions, the thought of the reality.
Entertain your mind (and be content) with whatever you get" - SC.

"Leave off the thirst to acquire wealth
Dispassionate in mind, gather thought of the Real,
What is gathered by yours own efforts and exertions
That wealth, own and enjoy to heart's content" – BS

2. Give up thirst

Cosmos, full of dynamism, always in the flux of change
the desires, greed and stormy realm of lust always changing
bringing worries, unhappiness, and sorrows to humans
the thrust to posses creating bondages
and the desires multiplying boundlessly.

The objects and wealth as such benign but
the desires returning ruthlessly with merciless tyranny
degrading men and women and bringing worries
strains, struggle and labor, painful gain and painful loss
anxiety to preserve, all this a game of the restless sorrows.
Give up the thrust to possess wealth, live the life of
detachment with intelligent and chaste relationships
the mind devoid of passions withdrawn from preoccupations
empty it to reapply in contemplation on the Eternal
discover a sense of contentment, live with what is acquired
labor with honor, live with honor to bring true happiness
to experience inner peace, renunciation bringing the true joy.

Discover new dimensions, higher contemplations
renounce worldly attachments and enjoy the spiritual reality
we being the inheritors of the eternal peace and perfection.

"Seeing the full bosom of young maidens and their naval do not fall a prey to maddening delusion, this is but a modification of flesh and fat, think well thus in your mind again and again"- SC.

"Viewing with lust at a Woman's waist and chest
Don't you be caught in vice of passions wild
Consider well, all this is naught, mere flesh and fat
Remember in your mind…again and again" - BS.

3. Lust

Give up lusty passions for women, lust for wealth
this irresistible urge of all 'intelligent' people
to possess more wealth and to enjoy women
to escape pain and to attain happiness
to end anxieties and have sense of security.

These possessions providing fences against the enemies
building imaginary fortresses around us with wealth—
millionaires wanting yet more and more, getting secured
bringing more happiness and enjoyment
more wealth, more power, false assurance of security.

With the fortress of security, what else to do?
to enjoy and attain more and more happiness, never realizing
the fall into ever irresistible downward spiral
of enchantments of the flesh
running after the bosom ('breasts'), perhaps
the most beautiful organs of women.

Both men and women attracted to each other in
a constant flux of wealth, for pleasure and pleasure for wealth
both earning the sorrows—the antithesis of happiness.

The urge of attraction being nature's act
the natural affinity for the charm of the opposite sex
the gift and need of the evolution - the process of
natural selection for procreation and prolongation
of the genes and species further for millions of years to come.

O! seeker of the Truth, regulate that natural urge
only the disciplined, purified, and sublimated mind
-intellect/intelligence-can achieve the pure state of consciousness.

Animals acting on their instincts, impulses cannot do this
only man with his rational thinking
from carnal to nobler and to more divine
can achieve this state of pure joy
by reversal of instincts and rational contemplation.

"The water-drop playing on a lotus petal has an extremely uncertain existence; so also is life ever unstable. Understand the very world is consumed by disease and conceit, and is riddled with pangs" -SC

"A dew-drop trembling from a lotus petal
So uncertain is the life...not known for how long!
The entire world that you see around, know,
Is full of dole, disease, and conceit" -BS

4. Dew-drops

Life as uncertain as the drop of water on the lotus petal
yet in the short period gets consumed by diseases and worries
you feel troubled by dozen pangs
the life being uncertain and the world full of sorrows
where is the time to waste?

Death not announcing its visit – enters the cities and houses
and work places—not respecting person, his/her status
place and position, his/her possessions and wealth
his/her might or even achievements, pride and fame.

All such achievements, possessions, aggrandizements
of no 'value' to the death, a stark and dark reality
to happen to every and all humans.

Strive from now and right now and right here
Lord Budha says the same thing - all here is misery and misery
all around, all is momentary and momentary
temporary and prone to vanishing.

The lotus grows 'out of water', in water it exists
nurtured and nourished by the very water
and ultimately it perishes in water
the flower an 'expression' of the water
and the seed of the flower
the manifestation of both the seed and water
the expression of the seed in the tree

the expression of the tree in the seed
cycle of the evolution within the seed and within the tree
the seed is in the tree and the tree in the seed
flower in the water and water in the flower.

The life of an individual thus disappears as easily as
the drop of the water falling in the water (of rive or ocean)
life merging into larger life wherever it exists in the Cosmos
if it exist at all – no body really knows.

Whether larger life (the Paramatma) exists or not
the smaller life anyway disappears
may be into something else, no body knows
or into just nothingness, into naught
into 'shunya', the null space.

May be the life comes from or springs up from pure nothingness
that initial existence being infinitesimally and infinitesimally
small and smaller to being nothingness
that could be so enigmatic and awesome reality
beyond the grasp of all the religions, all the philosophers
beyond all the knowledge, all the sciences
beyond all thoughts and all endeavors.

Yet it is so vivid that we live it and enliven to live and feel it
the true essence of the self, the life, since it makes us run
around and after our desires, makes us dance to its tunes
its vagaries keep us on our toes
it is never silent when it is here and there
but it becomes nothingness when it is not here and not there
but somewhere it would have been or must be
for it comes back and wakes you up in the morning
and gets done thousand tasks in your life.

It is spontaneous here and it seems all pervading
as if never going to extinct for ever and ever at all
seems omnipotent and all invigorating
that is life with its lively livingness nourishing
the lives of people and all the species in the cosmos.

"As long there is the ability to earn and save so long are all your dependents attached to you. Later on when you come to live with an old, infirm body, no one at home cares to speak even a word with you!"-SC.

"When money you earn, and are capable still
Your kith and kin see so much to love
Capacity lost, old and sick, you drag on stick
None to enquire your health even at home!!"-BS.

5. Nothing for Nothing

We are selfish, utterly selfish, even too selfish
'nothing for nothing' is the law of Nature working in evolution
and for evolution, works for even humans - more so in humans!

It seems universal that we are deferential to the earning
member of the family, the one who earns wealth is more
respected
and adorned by others around for the hope of
getting some benefits from the earning member.

The money begets money, the wealth earns more wealth
earns even respect and alas the absence of wealth is only
sorrow!
the age (-ing) saps away all physical and intellectual efficiency
the sad way of the world – shall all will leave the rich
once his capacities decay to earn and save.

Let you earn more, distribute more to your capacities
enjoy your wealth as much you want to your popularity
affection and reverence from others – knowing well
O! intelligent human, that this is not the final goal of the life
but to earn inner peace and self-tranquility
devoid of the influence of crowds, masses around us.

Be psychologically away from all crowds, vanities, conceits
and false values, the deceptive sense of security
the security obtained due to too much wealth.
Turn inwards from the outer world to your inner world
from the outer space to the inner space
from the extrovertedness to the introvertedness
from the outer expansion to inner contraction into
the inner microscopic world of your own that
infinitesimally small world of inner space – that itself
is really very vast, infinite in its quality, presence, and love
with infinite possibilities, avenues of the expansion of
our life to infinite care, affection, and love
that should and can embrace the entire humanity and
even more and more and for ever and ever!

Let you young strive, struggle, and adventure
let you earn, spend, and give, just as your hobbies
since the real goal for the life, for our lives, for us –
the humanity is the act of self-purification, to seek perfection
with inner personal contemplation
to embrace the entire humanity in our fold
whatever our folds that might be
we embrace the world before it disembraces us.

We reject the worldly activities before the world rejects us
we retire into the richer world of peaceful contemplation
the intense self-engagements, the meditative
intuitive serene contemplation.

"As long as there dwells breath (life) in the body so long as they
enquire of your welfare at home. Once the breath (life) leaves, the
body decays, and even the wife fears that very same body" —SC.

"Life pulsating still, when air moves in and out
Others make enquiries anxious of your health
Life gone, when body falls down dead and inert,
Even your wife, dear, fears to be near!" -BS.

6. Even wife fears

Let you not yourself overindulge in extrovert life
not live the life of pessimism, being aware of
the brittle vanities of life, live in service of human kind
to develop healthy introvertedness.

The Rishis of the yore had observed the life
with an ideal scientific detachment with a relentless honesty
with a shattering realism and depicted the life
to develop healthy optimism while shattering
old and false values, they very carefully substituted
with a set of healthier and more enduring values of
positive thinking and positive living.

The philosophers of the East seem to portray the life very dark
stark dreary and seem to drive away from humans
the incentive to live, enjoy and to progress
indeed they warn us that to spend our entire life time
in sheer body-worship, fashioning and earning more for
our vanities even at the cost of some 'lives' is futile and
abominable intellectual stupidity into which we easily sink to
our own peril.

We do need to sweat and toil, fight and procure to feed and breed, to cloth and shelter the body — it is the very body that needs all these to maintain it clean, young, strong, healthy it is this body through which we can act and do many mundane jobs — eat, smell, see, feel, and do several difficult tasks.

But to spend the entire life span and time in these alone is a criminal waste of our abilities, for the body ultimately will grow old tottering, infirm and then perish - for ever, never ever returning to this world — the biological fact, a profound truth — the same bodies/lives and the people, perhaps, do not come back
the new born come with their own-new-bodies only with their new tendencies —the bodies being mortal and not immortal.

To worship this body to its fullest and ignore the development of 'self' is utter ignorance and waste of one's precious life time it is wiser to end the attachment with the body and to really blast off all the futile vanities of our lives.

It is a profound truth that the animal bodies have some use after they are dead—the skins, bones used for making a few things but, alas, the human body does not have any apparent use—it has a nuisance value—unless some organs are donated to someone to see better, to throb better, to live better!

Otherwise, inherently the body is filthy and to maintain such a body you earn more and more wealth, hoard it, and 'cut' many throats, wage many wars!, and of the dead body of yours even your own nearest, dearest and your own spouse would fear!

126

O! disciple, O! seeker of the Truth, meditate on this bare fact of body's finite existence, get detached from the body-vanities.

But, keep it just clean, beautiful, feed it, clothe it
just do that with complete understanding of its function and
temporariness, and considering it as an instrumentation
live in the body with a healthy disregard for it!

"So long as one is in ones' boyhood, one is attached to play; so
long as one is in youth, one is attached to ones' own young woman
(passion); so long as one is in old age, one is attached to anxiety
(pang)...(yet) no one, alas, to the Supreme Brahman is (ever seen)
attached!!" - SC.

"A child thinks not of aught, but of its play,
A lad is engrossed in full in a youthful lass,
The old man with a glory and a gloom both past, has much to worry
Alas, no one is free to think of Him the Supreme" – BS.

7. Phases

Life is short, yet the pilgrimage to its goal very long and
many if not all tied down to the flesh, gold and wealth
suffer 'sweet-bitter' agonies in their lives.

Drunk with passions and lust, wandering away from the
main path, rambling into thorny bushes, bleeding and fatigued
eventually falling into the bottomless pit of death
this being the universal folly of all the humans.

Childhood days spent (wasted) with toys and games
natural to that age, the youth is spent in passion
for young women (and men) and lusty sports and
finally the age gathers, the gray hairs conceal our anxieties and
fears of the old age problems and
the very end, the death.

And alas, we do not get the time to get attached to the supreme
essence of life, the Almighty
we do not have time or we do not spend time to understand
the profound truths of life and their powerful illusions.

We do not read science and evolution to understand
the complexities and real beauty of the biological species
we do not ask right type of questions, from where are we
how are we hear, and why are we here, and what are we
supposed to do in this short span of our lives on this planet?

We are lost between various religions, waging wars even on
the bases of religions, and the people who even believe in 'God'
of one religion do not hesitate, do not waste time
to kill those who follow 'God' in other religions!
who can be so 'irrational' as humans—with their
so- called super intelligence!

Perhaps, it is only in humans that an irrationality can exist
for in plants and animal kingdoms there is no such
irrationality there is only the natural behavior based on
instincts!
the nature (the prakriti) is neither cruel nor kind
it is just indifferent
it is unfortunate that the humans with their declared super
intelligence and intelligent thinking can act so irrationally!

The birth and growth, play and passions, sorrows and pangs-
we the humans go through these cycles in our lives
the dolls and balls, passions for women, worries and anxieties
of old age and sufferings, and we did not get time to rationally
think about our selves, but we used our rational thinking for
technological developments, we rocketed to air and deep space
developed super fast trains, gadgets for pleasures and wars!

Alas, we spent not enough time in the pursuit of serious
studies about the life and its purpose, our extrovertedness but
is natural, yet cannot be forgiven for the humans

the other biological species governed by natural instincts
the humans have the inherent ability to think wisely
and act rationally, to analyze their inclinations, temperaments
tendencies, and judge their follies and limitations, and
reject these if found foolish and dangerous to humankind.

We can use our judgmental capability to the benefit of
ourselves as well as other of our kinds, even other species
we can rise above the mundane passions, greed,
aggrandizement, lust, utter selfishness, cruel thought of
looting and killing
our own types and kinds!—the parameters indicating
the fall of humanity, was never in such a state of peril
as is in the present times!

The humans, the roof and crown of things, only if we utilize
our intrinsic intellect and the gathered intelligence
of rational thinking and rational acts
then only can we reach the highest perfection
not only in our technological development but also in our
personal lives of achievements and
really be altruist in the real sense of the term.

May we get time to withdraw ourselves from such
preoccupations of the senses and
get time to seek the changeless and the immutable.

"Who is your wife? Who is your son? Supremely wonderful indeed
is this Samsar. Of whom are you? From where have you come? Oh
brother, think of that Truth here."- SC.

"Who is your wife and who is your son?
This world-of-changes, know, is a wonder of wonders
Of whom are you?...whence have you come?
Brother, think of the Truth...Here and now!"- BS.

8. Empirical samsar

Bonds of family, beneficial, can liberate man from
his ego-centric selfishness, and yet have limitation
the bonds not an end in itself
man and woman living together with mutual love and respect
honored parents and still have to learn from each other
in mutual association, true spirit of togetherness
and yet in the human follies, unhealthy state of attachment
grows to each other, that very balm becomes a poison.

Should we live in the spirit of togetherness, but with a little
space between the two for their independent development
for their own expansion of their individual personality and
talents, the clinging attachment being so unhealthy.

The family being the field of trials, tests, ordeals
ups and downs, a field ground to help the individuals grow
into healthier personalities, the home is the life's college giving
opportunities and avenues to the development of both together
and yet individually, independently and yet this college
regard not as the life's main field of achievement
it is natural for man and woman to live in attachment and
sink in the family mire, as duck takes to water.

Ask question who is your wife, who is your son and so on...
it is like a train journey, where people meet and live
temporarily together, chat, enjoy, rejoice and yet at some
moment part apart go to their own destinations and
engagements.

We come across each other at some point of time, we meet and
develop relations, some intense, some vague and then depart
die and vanish, the life to death an incredible journey
this very journey concept pointing us to have right attitude
to maintain a healthy relationship with each other as well
with the people around in the world.

Your son was only a fetus, only a seed in the mother's womb
her loins, the seed came from the food you eat and assimilated
the food from the Earth, the 'clod-of-Earth' went through
various manifestations to become the fruit—the food, the seed
the fetus then the child, and you and we all, the child being
the ultimate effect of the penultimate cause of the mud!

At the microscopic level one piece of 'mud' gets attached
to another one, the father gets attached to the son
how strange is the spell of the Maya-the illusion
the empirical life, the Samsar—the worldly life a fascination
that needs to be looked upon thoughtfully, analyzed
meditated upon, the enquiry would and should lead us to realize
the right kind of relationships with each other, our beloved
ones, our brethrens, many more, and more to come by and go by
in this enchanting and dynamically vibrant life on this planet.

O! brother, please contemplate, who we are, where we come from, what are our goals here while we are here for short span of our life, what should be our attitudes to things, other beings even the members of the other species
more so to hundreds of the events happening around us and develop the capacity to think rightly and act wisely.

"Through the company of the good, there arises non-attachment; through non-attachment there arises freedom from delusion; when there is freedom from delusion, there is the Immutable Reality; on experiencing Immutable Reality there comes the state of 'liberated-in-life'."- SC.

"Company of good leads to detachment true,
Detachment gets you past the delusion-dens
No longer deluded, the Changeless Reality dawns,
Experience of the Real gives the Liberation sure!"-BS

9. Company of good

Every hour in temptations of life and its worldly offerings to us the wealth and women being attractive engagements the objects of fascinations numerous, their enchantments too powerful, irresistible, the mighty sorcery of the sensuous world acting on to us rendering us meek to fight the onslaught of these.

The path to follow is to have company of 'good"
the company of good-thoughts within ourselves to help ourselves being safe from rising waves of the passions thus a fortress from our association with good people around us.

Often are we so careless in choosing the company, our friends our associations, the bad company sweeping us away into the powerful waves of blind passions.

To develop and be in the company of good – the good people –
the learned men and women of science and philosophy
the men of right actions, the righteous (men and women)
freedom fighters, the men and women of wisdom
the lovers of peace, the seekers of the Truth
the seekers of the highest, the teachers of the humanity.

Such assemblies of good humans creating a magical power
the congregation erecting a powerful fortress to protects us
from the powerful illusions of the world and
its mighty tentacles of passions, lust and greed
the company develops the sense of detachment, the ability to
withdraw from the sensuous fields of attraction.

In turn the delusion-the Moha-and all the delusory false
values gradually disappearing, the inert objects now not being
able to enchant the mind, the mind learns not to assign values
to such temporary aspects of worldly life.

We learn to see the things as they are–the profound truth
of the objects around us, their natural play, their illusions
becoming clear to us, the mind knowing this redeems from
its own desires the vasanas, and a glimpse of the immutable
reality is experienced by the mind.

As more and more of this glimpse- experience, more and more
wisdom in understanding the interplay of events and their
effects around us, more and more enlightenment about the self
ushers us into the arena of the 'liberated-in-life' leading us to
the state-of-steadfastness.

The delusion that is of the mind assigning values to temporary
aspects in life disappearing, the mind reaches steadfastness
and into the contemplative meditation, the peaceful and
serene state-of-mind, the calmness prevails, the restlessness
disappears the anxieties subside or vanish
leaving the mind devoid of thoughts of worldly possessions
passions, desires, lust, greed and it experiences
the space of expansion of nothingness to the full true state of
understanding of the world play, this nothingness instantly
connecting to the vast expansion of space, the vacuum, the
shunya, may be billions and billions and more years ago there
was only "nothing" (shunya) the space only.

The state of liberation-in-life is to experience this 'nothingness'
the empty space despite of existence of the billions of objects
and billions of people in this Universe, despite of hustle and
bustle in the world, sounds and noises around us.

This being rendered possible only thr' the process of intelligent
withdrawal of the mind from the objects of the world
and redeeming the mind and ourselves from the vasanas,
the mutable aspects, by intense intuitive contemplative
meditation.

"When the age (youthfulness) has passed where is lust and its play?
When water is evaporated, where is the lake? When wealth is
reduced, where is the retinue? When the Truth is realized, where is
Samsar?"-SC.

"Where is the passion's play when the youth is gone?
Or the lovely lake when the waters are dry?
Where is the relatives', retinue, when riches are reduced?
And where is the smothering world, when Truth is known?"-BS.

10. Where is the retinue?

When the muscles are hard and strong, the blood is stormy hot
the individual is young and hearty
the maddening lust of blinding passion remains
lust springing from the youthfulness.

Lake is not the lake when the water is evaporated
is a dry land, the bed of sand and soil
the waters of desires keeping the youth vigorously active
to fulfill the very desire.

When your wealth is reduced, your retinue disappears
when the truth is realized the worldly things
thoughts, attachments disappear
the empirical samsar is gone with the wind!

The perfection not reached due to the veil of the vasana-fumes
the ignorance, when the ignorance ends the empirical
phenomena of finite objects with their tyranny disappear.

Condition of our inner-life creates chaos of an ego
meaningless achievements and mad roaming of the
individuality when the inner vasana condition changes the
ego is eliminated when there is no ego, "perceived-felt-thought
of" recede into nothingness, just shunya, the experience of
the infinite space consciousness itself revealing as the state of
Truth
the individual consciousness and the universal consciousness
becoming the very nature of the seeker.

"Take no pride in your possessions, in the people (at your command), in the youthfulness (that you have). Time loots away all these in a moment. Leaving aside all those, after knowing their illusory nature, realize the State of Brahman, and enter into it".-SC.

"Gather not pride for youth, wealth and your hold on men,
Time, the tyrant, loots away all in a moment short,
Knowing all this as an illusion and a thick delusion,
Realize and enter the State that is of Supreme One!

11. Illusion

Slave to false vanities, hollow conceits, to the wheel of woes in samsar, the worldly changes and jerks, we humans get affected the relationships with the objects, feelings, thoughts through the body, mind and intellect creating false attitudes
"my people", "my things", "my joys", "my ideas"
we suffer from the finitude and the floods of changes
their enormous effects, all belonging to the world of objects.

Wealth, social connections and status, family status, youth and vigor become the pillars of upon which platform of sense enjoyment is built, yet the wealth moving from person to person the youth does not last long, the social status, popularity and power all are part of the people (Jana) and relations with them
all these based on the fancy and mood of the hour.

Seek the knower of it all, the very principle illuminating all the worldly experiences, realize this consciousness that presides over all our inner experiences, know it then as the infinite consciousness everywhere.

"Day and night, dusk and dawn, winter and spring again and again come (and depart). Time sports and life ebbs away. And yet, one leaves not the gusts of desires."-SC.

"Day and night …and the dawn and the dusk,
Winter and spring come and go round and round,
Time plays on and the life ebbs out,
But the gust of lust, know, leaves not one! – BS

12. Life ebbs

The day and night cycle through dusk and dawn, seasons come and depart, the time moves on, the future becomes the present and that too rolls away into the past, often forgotten.

The time never stops for no body and under no condition
being ever on a forward march, and we get bogged down by our
past memories, more so bad ones and less good ones, and
get excited for the future, and spent time, and mind on endless
roller-coasters affected by strides of time
our hopes and plans seem defeated being at the time's mercy
the life itself at time's mercy, we spend time to enjoy the sense
objects, striving, sweating and toiling endlessly to acquire
possess, aggrandize and hope to spend for our constant
happiness and the whirl- pool cycle continuing till death.

And the death snatches away every thing, we leave away
things here and here only, the creatures as we are, we sadly
and tragically depart leaving behind us, for others to enjoy and
rejoice, on our own efforts of life time!

*The glittering objects are rendered enchanting and more
attractive, beyond their own intrinsic appeal and appearance
of their natural beauty, by our mind and by our lust to acquire
and possess, we add false values to these objects and we
strongly feel that we need them, without which as if we would
die.*

*This imaginary joy in seeing objects' additional false beauty,
joy in acquiring, possessing and using them takes our life time
and entire effect distracting us away from the path of
self-realization, and we become blind to our
true state of perfection and consciousness.*

*The body decades, the life steadily ebbs away, the body becomes
infirm and yet the desires do not die or vanish-they even grow
the death crawls behind all of us, disease and decays
accompany us and we eventually reach the grave, all the time
worried and full of anxieties and still longing for
the joys of the glittering objects.*

*O! the seeker of Truth, be wise and wiser, and wiser giving
up the desires, seek the absolute reality, the almighty that lies
behind all the finite objects of the world, that is the inner life
and life giver to us that
infinite consciousness could satisfy us all.*

*O! disciple seek this absolute truth, infinite awareness and
be free from the bondages and passions of the world and its
objects.*

"Oh, distracted one! Why worry about wife, wealth, etc.? Is there not for you the One who ordains (rules, commands?). In the three worlds it is the 'association-with-good-people' alone that can serve as a boat to cross the sea of change (birth and death)."-SC

"Why this worry for woman and wealth,
Mad one! Isn't there one to ordain your life?
In the three worlds, know, the company-of-the-good
Is the only skiff that rows across the ocean-of-change!"-BS

13. Good association

Oh! the distracted seeker why you worry so much about (your) wife or wealth, the worries do not pay in life, worries waste our minds and energies, the disturbed mind gets stormed with sensuous thoughts, the poor mind has no vitality left and becomes weaker to face any challenges
the exhausted we become with sapped out of dynamism.

We fail not because the world is strong enough to break us, but because we are not strong enough and hence the world around us, the world of happenings around us is rendered more powerful and stronger than us, as is said the weak must and do perish almost always—being the golden law of nature.

To dissipate in sensuous thoughts is unholy
wife is more than a sensuous convenience
there is in her the concealed motherhood of all human-kind
she is the sanctity of the family institution and
true mother-hood, a practical reality that this motherhood
is the creation of the (subsequent) humanity
of all humans, men and women of the world, and perhaps in
the entire cosmos, on unexplored planets, unexplored universes
anywhere in the vast expanse
may be we cannot rule out such a possibility.

This institution of home, the sanctity of the motherhood in
the woman, the female sex, is perhaps the most fundamental
substratum for the humans
to live on this planet peacefully and enjoy the benefits provided
by the mother nature, the evolutionary experience.
The par excellence, extraordinaire, the highest kind of the
material–worldly bonanza, the most magnificent
the most wonderful, mind-blowing happening
that is this evolutionary experience, at least for those who are
ready and open-minded
to experience the fathomless vastness of the colorful cosmos.

To demean, to pull down such a sanctum sanctorum
the greatest institution of home and the motherhood
would be the peril of the entire human kind
o! seeker of the Truth, uphold such a pious and divine tradition
sans self-gratification, sans degrading, demeaning, and
devolutionary thought currents.

Curtail the routine ramblings of the mind, uplift the thoughts
to higher level, to higher consciousness, higher and greater
awareness by constant remembering of the Almighty
for there is no remedy from a fall if one fell into the deep
well of rut of thinking habit of exhausting one's personality,
vitality.

A definite hope to come out of such a self ruining habit and pit
of self-vanity is to be in a constant and continual association
with the good people, the well educated, self-controlled
women and men with vision and a mission
by continual association with them, the mind of the seeker of
the Truth gets channeled, his/her thinking also and ultimately
by shunning the old and odd habits, will be able to develop a

143

healthy attitude towards things, other human beings, giving a
new purpose and direction for our thought-life.

With the quality of thoughts changed for the better, we shall
discover in our self a new inspiration within us
to propel us to push ourselves to more rewarding fields
day by day we will be able to strive for the higher and higher
to the state of Godhood of Love—GOL, the picture of
the GOL becoming much clear.

The physical self control bringing the mental peace leads to
satisfying inner joy of the (spiritual) heart
the inner instrument paving the way for sincere self-study and
reflection, leading to the assurance of credible profit of
living in the spirit of GOL.

The earlier the better, the more the merrier, the more the better
contact with the good, association with the good
all beneficial through our life for the continual
self development and growth within (ourselves).

The company of spiritual teachers, and co-students will help us
on our pilgrimage, the good-association
becoming our boats to cross the ocean of many worldly
limitations and the sea of change
the constant association with the wise
becoming a protective armor to our inner-equipment
our only armaments which we can use to fight the onslaught of
our own false values and acquired habits of sensuous living.

"One ascetic with matted-lock, one with shaven-head, one with hairs pulled out one by one, another parading in his ochre-robes- these are fools who, though seeing, do not see. Indeed these different disguises or apparels are only for their belly's sake."-SC.

"Matted locks, the shaven heads, and the plucked hair,
Diverse, the guises in saffron robe,
The fool sees it, but perceives not,
All guises are, indeed devices to fill the belly big!"-BS

14. Seen, yet not seen

Some body, thousands of years ago, did not want to work
hence inaugurated the art of killing, with the motive of
obtaining maximum benefits with minimum effort, more food
and the destruction of civilization, perhaps started with
the concept of minimum labor and maximum comfort, and
the man sank to immoral, unethical, and barbarous status
these human instincts having remained true to this day
to be idle and is seen more in our times
the history has witnessed these idle shams in plenty at all the
levels of society, in all departments of activity
some even would have escaped to Sanyas for these reasons
seeking and finding happier life, they might bluff the
generations and play upon the credulity of the people.

With such instincts, a few politicians, governors and even
priests, Sadhus, Bhagats, Sanyases, might tend to be more
burdensome to the societies, if they outplay their roles away
from their respective spheres, circles, and their private lives.

145

Unfortunately we suffer their wrong-doings as royally and
nobly as we suffer the great natural disasters
like floods, blizzards or volcanic eruptions, their angers
over-claims, effects of their wrong decisions, policies
short-term and long-term effects of wars and so on.

It is unfortunate, but it is largely true, that such self-deceivers
wear often the same uniform and garbed in the similar/same
clothes as done by the real gurus (true Sanyases)
the copiers, the fakes wear the matted locks, shaven heads, and
colored ochre clothes, and so on
such fake ones, look or pose as real ones, are found in various
religious places, even in times now as was the case during the
times of Shankaracharya that he himself vividly points out here
what a spectacular continuum of the natural instincts of
minimum labor and maximum benefits.

Some spot very long beards, long hairs, and long robes, keep
long sticks, painted foreheads, and call themselves sanyases
and followers of one or other cult, or religion or
path of self-realization, and are often half-learned, ill-
informed of the real philosophy or true tenets of even their own
religions.

In fact we all humans, from this point of view have half
backed knowledge, since the knowledge is infinite in quantum,
quality and scope, this infinite knowledge no one can ever
grasp in one life and we require several lives, may be an infinite
numbers of lives (an impossible task any way)
but with this half backed status, imperfect knowledge, if we
do not cheat and deceive the innocent people of our societies,
then it is and would be a great service to the society.

Be as much humble/honest as possible, lest we would be on the wrong path away from true self realization, estranged from the true path of service to the society, forgetful of our real goal to attain perfection and status of GOL, the Godhood of Love.

These different disguises only serving us to fill our belly and not satisfying our philosophical seeking of the truth guided by self-preservation, instincts, lust for power, show-off, display of wealth, more false-hood would prevail in the society than ever before.

Unfortunately thus we have more false leaders, watch dogs artists, preachers, and so on in our society than ever before the falsehood is unfortunately as much a brilliant human capacity and a device as the honesty is human's one of the heroic perfections, it is unfortunate that such deceptions are prevalent all over the world and in many walks of our lives, in some pockets : creeds, political, economic, scientific and even spiritual arena.

Interestingly, intellectually such persons are aware of and knowing what is the noblest way of life—they see it and yet they fail to live up to it—they do not see it.

Such people are liability to the society, and they live in this way only to live easy life and for their belly, a well paid profession of deception, the whispers of the lower passions become more urgent than the call of (from) the higher-aspirations, the desire catching up again here.

"The body has become worn out. The head has turned grey. The mouth has become toothless. The old man moves about leaning on his staff. Even then he leaves not the bundle of his desires."-SC

"Body worn out, and hairs turned silver white,
Teeth gone, mouth gaping round like a hollow cave!
The old man totters with a stick in hand,
Even he, leaves not the bundle of his desires!"-BS

15. Old age

The dilapidated physical form, the body tottering with the age and yet not ridden of all passions, the thirst and hunger for flesh is not yet gone, and for pleasures too
the mind is yet thirsty, the intellect does higher level planning yet the body cannot execute/implement the plans.

We in the prison cells of our mind's desires dream of our home moments of joy with our family and yet we cannot escape physically from behind the bars
the older we become the harder it becomes, the gapping distance between desires and the state of fulfillment
by the body sense organs ever increases
the older are we, we go through tyrannies of such inexpressible desires that ever chase us and storm us within and the ensuing conflict leaves us in the state of agonizing life
telling unimaginable sorrows.

We should cultivate the habit of controlling the desires even at our younger age, so that when we grow we can still live without agonies and with tranquility and inner joy.

Growing old, our hairs grow grey, or we loose all hairs towards
baldness, we loose teeth, fort-less tongue (but it will be happy
not being crushed between the hard teeth)
we move with the support of stick, lean and bend down as
old stuff, as we become older loosing the strength of our bones,
and joints, and keep dragging ourselves on the tottering legs
displaying our sad (and pitiable) state of existence
and yet we cannot leave behind the heavy dose and load of
desires, ironically and intriguingly, these desires multiply as we
grow older and older—this being the Maya-the net of illusions
the attachment without any achievements
the powerful illusion in our lives.

"In front of the fire, at the back of the sun, late at night he sits with his knees held to his chin; he receives alms in his own scooped-palm and lives under the shelter of some tree and yet, the noose of desires spare him not!"-SC

"Fire in front and the sun at the back,
The chin clasped to his knees on a chilly night,
Gathering alms in hollow-of-palm, and living under a tree
Yet even he, know, leaves not the rope-of-desire that binds!"-BS

16. Pseudo Sanyasi

The tyrannies of the desire being universal do not spare even
a wandering monk, as if the law of nature for the humans,
the gift of evolution to the humans, irrespective of their
personality and status spares no one
and here is wandering monk, saffron-robe clad or fully naked
apparently having renounced everything, the clothing, shelter,
and living only on minimum food—he still may need some shelter
to avoid onslaught of rains and scorching heat of Sun, and
cold nights and need fire to heat up in wintry nights.

Though accepting what is given, since he has left everything
worldly possessions behind him, looking like an ascetic, a man
of renunciation and yet the chords of desire never leave him
mere asceticism does not seem to be sufficient, renunciation of
only objects of the world is not going to work
the desires still working their devils.

A real sacrifice and drying of desires is called for much at the
early stage of life, at younger age of youthfulness, to learn to
curb the desires to escape the shackles of their powerful grip
and craving for them, the goal is to attain total elimination
mere and just self-denial is not enough
it should be accompanied by a high mental purity

how much sincere denial and renunciation, if not accompanied
by non self-indulgence, would bring self-destruction
only physical self-denial being not enough
the asceticism calls for total elimination of desires from the
mind, the asceticism be redirected for creative self-application
reapply the energy to the positive development and
spiritual unfolding, the sublimation of our instincts
there is no profit greater than sublimation.

"One may in pilgrimage go to where Ganges meets the ocean, called the Gangasagar, or observe vows, or distribute gifts away in charity. If he is devoid of first-hand-experience-of-Truth, according to all schools of thought, he gains, no release, even in hundred lives."-SC

"Pilgrimage pious to Ganges and sea, penances severe,
Charity in plenty, avail him not, all schools say;
He who hasn't got the knowledge of the Self,
Has no release from bonds in a hundred lives!"-BS

17. No release with charity

Unintelligent tapas (sacrifices) are unprofitable, without the knowledge of the Infinite reality and
liberation from our sense of finitude is impossible
the liberation from the sorrows of life cannot be gained
without actual first hand experience of the one Infinitude
the mere practice of pilgrimage to the holy river taking a dip or two into waters of such rivers and oceans, observance of vows, or distributing gifts for charity, are still superficial signs of renunciation, though in themselves the nobler exercises.

But one cannot reach the destination (even in hundred lives of oneself) without the true experience of oneness.

Of life-pilgrimage, this involves planning, executions, and some sacrifices, all giving vivid experiences and vitalizes our minds, if practiced with faith, dedication, and devotion, and sincerity
involves some sacrifices, tapas (if undertaken on feet, as they (devotees) might have done in the past, and yet many do now in the presence).

Educate your intellect (redirect or concentrate your intellect) to hold higher ideals, train your mind to obey your will, sharpen your will itself, control your sense organs, train them so that they cannot have everything they want.

The pilgrimages, vows, charity if carried out/practiced with a good purpose in mind become good exercises to prepare our minds for the great path of meditation and yet we cannot get total freedom from our natural weaknesses until through meditation we reach the highest goal.

Wake up oh! the limited ego, the individual seeker, and realize your infinite nature which has neither matter nor spirit.

"Sheltering in temples, under some tree, sleeping on the naked ground, wearing a deer-skin, and thus renouncing all idea-of-possession and thirst-to-enjoy, to whom will not dispassion bring happiness?"-SC

"Sheltered under trees in the House of God,
Earth alone for bed and deer skin for dress,
Renouncing all thirst for possession and enjoyment
Such a dispossession as this…how can it bring aught but joy?"-BS

18. Real renunciation

In this world even emperors are sorrowing, rich are worried, powerful people are anxious and as such all seem unhappy one points to other and feels the other is lucky and happy.

A truly renounced man may be without shelter, may be even without clothes, may be resting on a barren ground, may be he is wrapped in a deer skin, self- sufficient unto himself is independent of the world outside, who has discovered an inexhaustible fountain of joy and a rich treasure of true satisfaction in her/his own deep within in such a mental mood who will not be happy?

The inner richness may lead to one with outer poverty and yet there in our soul, the Emperor of all the Emperors lives the luxurious roughness of the ground, under some nameless and dry tree, in the courtyard of some temple and during the night when nobody is in the surroundings he is enjoying a perfect solitude.

He sleeps in a great comfort of purity of his heart
a true man, a true seeker, being innocent, has no mental
worries he shows peaceful love to all, he comfortably sleeps in
the luxury of his own purity and goodness
the real greatness of any human being.

"Let one revel in Yoga or let him revel in Bhoga. Let one seek enjoyment in company or let him revel in solitude away from the crowd. He whose mind revels in Brahman, he enjoys...verily, he alone enjoys."-SC

"Merged in meditation or merry in enjoyment,
Mixed in company or marooned in solitude,
Whose mind revels in Supreme One, constant,
His is the Bliss!...his indeed, is Bliss, his alone the Bliss!"-BS

19. Steadiness

Mind is the temple of joy when at rest, there is no joy when the
mind is chalked with desires, passions and attachments
in such a stormy surface, joy cripples, not fully experienced
a man of true realization, whether he is practicing yoga or
practicing bhoga (self indulgence), be in a company of the world
or be in his own loneliness
in a cave he alone still will be enjoying the full joy within.

He does not seek any joy from the outer world
he can have special powers to take certain decisions
in a human society some such committed dedicated good people
are given special powers, since they will not misuse, since they
will be even just good and noble
they will make just good decisions.

A man in the service of selflessness, a man of perfection can
still enjoy the world of objects, if he wishes to do so
by very nature a man of perfection cannot act against
the moral harmony and the ethical goodness in/of the society
such a man alone enjoys the spotless joy of being in the
Infinite.

"To one who has studied the Bhagvad Geeta even a little, who has sipped at least a drop of Ganges-water, who has worshipped at least once Lord Murari, to him there is no discussion (quarrel) with Yama, the Lord of Death."-SC

"He that catches the least glimpse of the Song of God,
He that tastes the least drop of the Ganges, - Eternal,
He that worships with least surrender the Destroyer-of-Mura,
Him, the Lord of Death even, dares not to discuss."-BS

20. Death dare not

There is no discussion with (the Lord of) death
may be you do not fear death
if you have done exercises for your spiritual unfolding
like the study of the Geeta, the holy book
if you have sipped the water of the Ganges and
if you have done the worship of the Almighty.

Worship of Murari signifies the annihilation of the human ego
to enter the glorious state of Immutable peace
the body consciousness and the ego-sense having arisen out of
false association with the matter, know, these to be shunned
away by devoted worship at the alter of the destroyer of ego
realize that the life within is the life everywhere
the seeker who has accomplished all these studies
the study of the Geeta, the spiritual scriptures (the Shastras)
striving and making the sincere efforts to reach the goals
to him the fear of death is remote
there is no need of any discussion of death, there is no fear at
all with the Lord of death, the Yama (the great controller of
death).

This principle of death is efficiently working all around the very " creation" is the continuous process of annihilation the cycle of birth and death is the process of "creation", "existence", and " annihilation" (in fact can be regarded as evolution!)

To create is to annihilate the present conditions of the living beings/things, to transform into new things, new beings, into new forms, shapes, sizes, features and presenting into a new condition, an extraordinary phenomenon of "evolution" .

If you live longer and longer and yet longer you will be tired of being in the same place, same condition, with the same or similar kind of people and situation, and older you become and the longer you live, the life will be filled with innumerable diseases and agonies unlimited.

It is in fact better and correct that the 'old'' and 'worn out' vanish naturally in the process of evolution and some other new born come to the life, with different outlooks, approaches, and methods, with new spirit, new enthusiasm and new ideas, and contribute their part and might-efforts to the existing conditions, situations, and again they vanish and the cycle goes on, bringing new avenues, new vistas, and throwing new lights on the phenomena of the world of the nature, bringing new understanding and creating awareness for the existing people, so that their consciousness is raised beyond what is/was at the present time.

The real ascetic does face the death, he does die one day but
presently and ever he does not fear death
he is in the realm of Infinite existence
he does not question death, does not fear death, nor does the
principle of death chase him ever or ask any question to him
the discussions and arguments of death are then un necessary
and not worth applying our minds and laboring any effort
since it being regarded as the principle of change
the inevitable one.

*"Again birth, again death, and again lying in mother's womb-this
Samsar process is very hard to cross over. . .Save me, Murare (Oh!
Destroyer of Mura, the ego) through Thy Infinite Kindness."-SC*

*"Once again the birth, once again the death,
Lying in mother's womb once again, helpless,
Difficult is this world-of-changes to get over,
Mercy, O Killer-of-Mura! save me from this!"-BS*

21. Cycle of birth

*The wheel of birth and death is restless for the living beings
never stopping for millions of years
our egos are enriched by our desires, our habits if/yet not
fulfilled, keep recurring and not leaving us yet
the process being difficult to overcome
ignorant we are of the ways of the world, our goals leading to
the extrovertedness and attachments to the objects of the world.*

*When we are born and when we grow, we have/develop our
own tendencies which bind us to the objects
which look beautiful and charming to us
all in fact is the creation of the Maya, the illusion at its best.*

*The real way is to live up to the natural tendencies and
to exhaust them away completely through rightful and
meaningful actions, these actions being undertaken without ego
and ego-centric desires, thus and so that no
newer tendencies precipitate and bother us.*

*Act and achieve with our actions, with the attitude of
dedication, with an idea to serve and in the spirit of Yagna
with the tendencies reduced, the thoughts become more calm
disturbances are reduced, the subtle body-
the combine of mind and intellect dies a mystic death*

it transcends to the blissful experience of the Infinite Spirit.

The tendencies gone, the thoughts gone, no subtle body there
to play the game of cycles of birth-and-death, no new birth is
required to give the platform to exhaust the tendencies, when
the old desires gone, controlled, or annihilated and no new
desires are born, there is no need for the instruments (body, etc.)
which are required to carry out the satisfaction of these desires.

Birth is as such painful (more to the mother though) and more
so is the death for everybody and we are helpless as such
and we are governed by the ego, the powerful force
the ego born of/from us, and yet starts ruling over us
and so relentlessly that it makes us, the 'I', the slave of it and
we need to free ourselves from this mighty tyrant, the ego
we need a mightier friend, a powerful and sympathetic friend
the rescuer, the savior, that destroyer of ego is the Almighty.

We at times are fatigued in life by the hardship, vagaries of life
meet wall with no hope of any kind, we struggle, sweat and
tears roll out of our eyes, our selfish acts stink and we are not
able to break the chords of our attachments and beaten out and
exhausted thoroughly and we feel helpless and where do we go?
– we seek grace from heavens....

*"The Yogi who wears but a godadi (a quilt) who walks the path
is beyond merit and demerit, whose mind is joined in perfect
Yoga with its goal, he revels (in God-consciousness)-and lives
thereafter-as a child or as a madman."-SC*

*"Covering the shoulders with a quilt of discarded cloth,
Following the path, bereft of both merits and de-merits,
The sage, his mind fixed, on the Supreme One, ever,
Revels constantly like a child, or a mad one!!"-BS*

22. Beyond merit

*He is not a child, a mad man, or a ghost and yet he looks like
one or lives like one, for he bears some qualities of a child, or a
mad man, or a ghost—his mental attitude to the world is that
of the detachment to the objects of the world.*

*He is the man who has renounced everything in the world
he wears only a 'godadi', having liquidated his own personality
a child expresses all kind of emotions and forgets all these
emotions in a moment, it does not drag past into present
it lives in its immediate happy moods
a perfect spontaneity in a child as well in a perfect seer
the Yogi, leaving in a chaste present from moment to moment
with no regrets carried on from the past and no anxiety for the
future, the man of realization lives right now here like a child.*

*We cannot enter the mind of a mad man, he is always in his
own mood, his own thoughts, and in the same way as a Yogi
Yogi while still walking and living amongst us, revels in his
own thoughts- so deep to understand (or even not able to
understand him at all) and gauge by us, he is above us, though
with his feet on ground his thoughts are above the clouds, the
likes and dislikes, ego and vanities, joys and sorrows, for he
revels in the peaceful state being in the great equipoise.*

He walks the path of inner life, which is beyond merit and demerit, good and bad, pleasure and pain, he is beyond the worldly dual, for him there is no description, prescription, and prohibition, he moves fearlessly in forests and quite places, day and night, fears no body, but others fear him, are afraid of him, with due reverence, he is like ghost who is afraid of none but all fear him- the ghost, the Yogi.

The child, the mad man, the ghost in him is no more a slave to his own body and his body does not demand anything he wears a simple godadi only for minimum protection.

"Who are you? Who am I? From where did I come? Who is my mother? Who is my father? Thus enquire, leaving aside the entire world-of-experiences, essenceless and a mere dreamland, born of imagination."-SC

"Who are you?...who am I?...Whence are we?
Who is my mother?...Who is the father?
Enquire thus within, casting off the non-essential...
The world entire...the phantasy of a mere dream!"-BS

23. Who am I?

Enquire the sources from which we might have arisen, by our rational intellect, who are we, from where we have come, how are we here, where are we all bound to be?
to gain and have true appreciation of the reality.

Not being able to do this enquiry, for we are busy dissipating our energies in mundane things, preoccupied with the happenings in the world (Vishwam), without realizing that all this is the result of our imagination
all that is to perish, is unreal, even the waking state of experiences are as unreal as dream state experiences.

Enquire into one's own self, the inner self to reveal the emptiness and hollowness of our own world of names and forms of the empirical world, of the enticing attachments and the empty vanities of the life that we live.

"In you, in me and in (all) other places too, there is but one All-pervading Reality. Being impatient, you are unnecessarily getting angry with me. If you want to attain soon the Vishnu-status, be equal minded in all circumstances."-SC

"In you and me and everywhere else is He, All-pervading,
Impatient with me, do not be angry and wrathful in vain,
Learn, in all places and all times, to be of equal-minded,
If, ere long, you wish to be one with Him!"-BS

24. Equal minded

Thousands of the masters at varied times for thousands of
years in Indic years (thousands years ago) experienced the
Eternal Truth that is in you, and me and in all, and
in all other places, one and one all pervading Reality.

Repetition is the part of life, the very essence of the universe
repeated moments, life and death, and then life and death
again destruction and construction, and rotation, revolutions-
within the matter and outside the matter, in microscopic
universe and celestial universe- there are repetitions,
movements and iterations and all that goes on and on.
The science is studied by repetitions, told in repetitions, and
conveyed again and again-the truth is conveyed by
the process of analysis and repetition to assert and convince
the people-the external truth is conveyed only thus.

We need patience to listen to this truth, we need
to read and listen the knowledge again and again
to fully understand, and our biological brains
(the natural neural networks) work in this way only
they are fed with the data, information, knowledge
previous learning again and again to learn the new patterns

to upgrade the old knowledge, to gain the confidence
by memorizing the vistas of facts and knowledge
-taking always a finite time and we all need to have
lot of patience, until we realize the perfection
we need to bear repetition.

To know the holy books of scriptures and their contents is
intellectually enriching, to appreciate the Infinite reality is
satisfying, however to experience it is another thing
following the logic in these books, and appreciating the said
existence, is thrilling and gratifying, but it is not sufficient
though for a seeker (an ordinary one) it is a must.

But to accomplish all that solely in our own heart and
experience and feel the subtlety of the higher planes
of consciousness and awareness, is the real experience
all that can be gained by practicing equanimity of the mind
to remain unshaken, practice even-mindedness.

And this is achieved by dedicated actions, devotion to almighty
service of/to mankind, contemplation upon the highest and
constant study and reflection, the constant even-mindedness
both in desirable and undesirable circumstances
the equal vision on all things and all times
being the very essence of Yoga.

Once the equanimity of mind mastered - the experience of the
infinite shall descent in us and
we will attain the status of Liberation-in-Life (LiL).

"Strive not, waste not your energy to fight against or to make friends with your enemy, friend, son or relative. Seeking the Self everywhere, lift the sense-of-difference (plurality), born out of ignorance."-SC

"A friend?...a foe?...The son?...or a relative?...
Beware!...befriend, not the one, nor contend the other-
Seeing your own Self in one and all, excepting none,
Root out all distinction, ruthless and firm, out of your mind."-BS

25. Beyond plurality

In and through every cell in my body, I live all spots, all times, and moments of varied experiences-I exist
even if my tongue suffers the tyranny of my teeth
I cannot and do not punish my teeth
I have no special relationship to any part of my body
I equally love all of them.

When the entire universe is emerged out from one Reality
who is there other, whom I can afford to hate?
all being the different manifestations of the one
and only one reality, who is special to love or to hate at all!

Hence strive not, do not waste energy to fight against anybody
or make friends with anyone, experience the oneness in
the universe, the mutual affinity, and rhythm of mutual
relationship of the universe which is held by a web of love.

In a loveless life of hate and meanness, littleness of heart and
limited view point there is suffocation, sorrow and agitation
hence expand and shift your attention to
the central source of beauty and eternal song.

*Develop vision to look beyond the externals of life and
look for the one substratum, the chord of beauty and truth
rise above the sense of differences
you are your own enemy and your own friend.*

*Once we experience the oneness with the absolute reality
there is no sorrow no delusion.*

"Leaving desire, anger, greed, and delusion, the seeker sees in the
Self, 'He am I'. They are fools who have not Self-Knowledge and
they (consequently), as captives in hell are tortured."-SC

"Desire and hunger, greed and delusion...one in the wake of the other,
Leaving all, the seeker sees the Self in Self,
Know, fools devoid of Knowledge-of-Self, get badly baked
In self-created prisons of Hell, born of ignorance!-BS

26. Here am I

Our knowledge of the outer world is objective, and
we understand and like to understand all that
other than ourselves
the spiritual experience when attained, the seeker feels it as
"He am I", and "That am I".

It is the process of discovering the realization of the self
the self-realization-the removal of the curtain of the total
ignorance-there is not anything like getting it, or obtaining it
since it was never lost, it was here and here only
but in our ignorance we did not realize
that it was here and here only.

It was our state of the mind that was not yet ready
not prepared to receive that knowledge
our thoughts were not ready to experience that state
of pure knowledge, the truth, our true self
the truth that all of us are
is concealed under our own ignorance of existence.

When the passions of the heart are removed
the Truth is self evident
know that as eternal sweetness of perfection

those who have not realized this (Atmagnyan) - the self
knowledge-live in sorrowful misunderstanding
they live as if living in a hell, a self-made hell
they think life is full of sorrows, perspiring passions
exhausting (fatigue –giving) desires and endless sentiments.

Due to misapprehension of ego, greed and anger
likes and dislikes, they live tortured by waves of passions
suffer eternally in a self-condemned existence
in a sort-of-hell created by themselves for themselves!

Assert your real mature, and realize the oneness of life
within yourself, and everywhere else.

"Bhagwad Geeta and Sahasranama are to be chanted; always the form of the Lord of Lakshmi is to be meditated upon; the mind is to be led towards the company of good; wealth is to be distributed (shared with) the needy."-SC

"Chant constantly, the Geeta of the Lord, and His 'thousands names',
Remember constantly the form of Sripathi, the Supreme Lord,
Lead constantly the unruly mind to the company of the good,
Give constantly the wealth that you have, to the deserving poor.

27. Free the mind

A spiritual program and agenda is advised
four aspects to be practiced
study the Geeta, worship the Lord-Almighty
cultivate the company of good, and serve the needy.

Bhagwat Geeta is a summary of the Upanishadic Truth
which should be regularly studied until fully understood
bringing reorientation in our intellectual outlook
on life, explaining the goal and the path
also try to live these ideas diligently and subjectively
experience the truth, the philosophy enumerates the ideals and
supplies with the logical sequence of thinking
to help the contemplative minds to appreciate their
implications -religion without philosophy is a superstition (and
philosophy without religion is/could be a lunatic dream).

Next is to learn to surrender at the altar of the Almighty
to the Almighty himself/herself
integrating the inner personality and lifting our mind high
above its ordinary status to acquire noble qualities.

And next is the company of good to constantly warm up
our enthusiasm to live up to our ideals and set out goals
we should live up to these ideals while in daily contacts
of the men and women around us-we should practice charity
to respect other man's need, and encompass
a wider circle of brotherhood in our own folds.

"Very readily one indulges in carnal pleasures, later on, alas come diseases of the body. Even though in the world the ultimate end is death, even then man leaves not his sinful behavior."-SC

"Easy is the plunge of the man into carnal pleasures,
In their wake, alas follow quick the ailments and the ills,
The end of life, though is but an embrace with death
He learns not by his sinful acts, nor does he mend!"-BS

28. Ultimate is death

Man easily falls and slips down the slopes of a mountain
evolution is all efforts, struggle, sweat and suffering
to live in flesh is universally easy for all
since for the flesh (Genes!) to crave constantly and
to live in sense gratification no practice is needed.

We need to give a heroic fight against our lower instincts and
win a divine mastery and supremacy over the flesh
to fight the tyranny of the genes
excessive self-dissipation bring suffering, only pains,
disabilities, faculties slowing down, and eventually decaying
and
the man tumbles to his grave, and yet we leave not our
sinful behavior, the vigorous push and pull of the vasanas
the Maya (illusion) pushes us into sin and pulls away from
our attempts of living a nobler life.

"Wealth is calamitous, thus reflect constantly: the truth is that there is no happiness at all to be got from it. To the rich, there is fear even from his own son. This is the way of wealth everywhere."-SC

"Disastrous is wealth, it gives not the least of joy
Know this to be true and keep ever in view,
'one attached to wealth...fears even his son' know-
This is the ordained way everywhere for all!"-BS

29. Wealth illusion

There is no true happiness to be got from wealth
even the rich fear their own kith and kin
the Maya-fascination for what money promises to procure is
very powerful, the man discovered the money but
became slave to it, the money rules on everybody.

Money has a value, but do not give over-exaggerated
importance to it, lest it will breed lovelessness, hatred and
subhuman impulses, pushing us to play the grabbing games,
becoming jealous of others who have more than us
profit-hunting instincts growing more powerful and
the vicious cycle is set on.
The money is only a means and not an end-in-itself
just have in sufficient measure to use for
what you wanted and employ in your service
when you possess, it is a blessing
when it possesses you, it is a curse.

This is the truth about the wealth all over the world
intriguing and amazing way of the wealth.

"The control of all activities (of life's manifestations in you), the sense withdrawal (from their respective sense-objects), the reflection (consisting of discrimination between the permanent and the impermanent), along with Japa and practice of reaching the total-inner-silence, these perform with care...with great care."-SC

"Control of life's Pranas; withdrawal of senses from their objects, Japa, and discrimination of things permanent and impermanent-
Quietening the mind through means of meditation-
Do with care! with great care! extreme care!"-BS

30. Total inner silence

Control all subjective activities within your own personalities control activities in the body, practice sense-withdrawal and discrimination, japa and reaching a state of utter silence within.

Pranayam is not only a breath control actually it means to have control of five physiological systems roll the mind back to himself, develop a discriminating attitude and intellect to see permanence beyond impermanent to be repeatedly done by constant scientific thinking.

Repeated pre-thinking, training of the mind then the mind/thoughts become steady and gain the capacity of understanding the subtler and deeper suggestions of the Upanishadic declarations.

Develop the discriminative power and gain the dexterity in withdrawing the mind from the unreal at all the levels of the personality (of the seeker)

tuning the mind to the highest, avoiding the disturbance from
the flesh-attractions, contemplate on the highest
the Real and reach the state of relative thoughtlessness.

The final experience is already within, only the veil of darkness
of ignorance, of limited tendencies, is lifted to reveal
the true nature of ours, the Eternal nature of Infinite
perfect tranquility, peace, purity and perfection.

These exercises are done with an artistic poise and
not by artificial suppression with hurry
hurry is also not so much in the nature
the evolutionary processes are damn slow, gradual.

Unfolding and learning step by step
iteration by iteration, repetition by repetition
many and perhaps all these processes take time to evolve
hence all these practices be performed with care and great care.

"Oh! Devotee of the Lotus-feet of the Teacher! May you become liberated soon from the Samsar through the discipline of the sense-organs and the mind. You will come to experience (behold) the Lord that dwells in your own heart."-SC

"O devotee of the Lotus feet of the teacher!
may you soon the forces of worldliness defeat,
And controlling the mind and the Sense organs well,
Perceive the One Supreme dwelling in your heart!"-BS

31. In your own heart

Faith is very powerful, secret and sacred source of energy
in our bosom
the logic of the discourses of the teacher helping us
intellectually comprehend the essence of the truth.

Hold on to what you intellectually believe
to see it in just near future, if you do not see it now
this might take us to our destination
have faith in the teacher of the truth
you may get liberated- in-life itself by disciplining
the sense organs and mind, here and here only
not in remote future, right here, and right now
in your own heart, you might come to experience
the Almighty who dwells in your own heart.

75. In my rhythm

If the night was such a great experience then it would
lead to more beautiful dawn and much brighter day
with all the stars disappeared, the darkness melted and
all the dreams vanished, the dawn with new hope will usher.

The birds came out chirping and signing the songs of eternity
the travelers are on their new journeys treading new paths
to where and why in this unknown world, they only know!

Your face is like the Moon with a star on its forehead and
you expand my horizon to infinity, to infinite peace
into the realm of pure beauty, serenity and love.

All spanning oceans of the world taking in your fold the
entire micro and macrocosm, your two eyes like the Sun and the
Moon beacon to the goals yet unattained for
the entire humanity.

If you are such a stunning beauty with magnificent personality
then how much greater will be your 'creator'?
If you are such a grace and purity then how much
great your 'creator' would be?

When you do not arrive, the search is on with bright eyes
wide open with doubts, what would happen otherwise!
when I get any trouble, my mind wanders and
fears if our relationship would break.

You are monsoon and I am clouds
you are the dawn and I am the evening
the entire world is asleep and the time is dancing.

I was never earlier ever so much happy than today
is it the coincidence or the (fate) nature's plan
that we met today, our paths are now joined and united
this moment had never occurred ever earlier in my life
will this dream be completely fulfilled?

Your village is a real beauty and your beauty is magnificent
and the Moon is bright and young and am stunned
with the colorful flowers that have blossomed
you are unknown to me, but now got engrossed and
engaged into you as if I knew you for ages.

If you sing along with me, along with my rhythm
with your mind into mine and to my company
our lives would be more fulfilling.

In the moonlit nights, hand in hand with me
if you sing and smile along with me
the life would be more enchanting.

If you sing in my rhythm, in my melody then
where is need to borrow happiness from the outer world?
if we sing together then we can enrich our souls
and reside in the eternal happiness and peace.

76. Radiance of intellect

It illuminates thoughts and feelings—in humans
the thought that I am happy-am aware of ideas and my
actions
the light of intellect illuminates our all faculties
we see our deeds and their actions.

We can see our follies and mistakes
we know where we went right or wrong
we feel this and all that around us
and are aware of all this
because constantly we live in this radiance
alas, still often we remain ignorant
of and do not register our mistakes.

This radiance is the aura of our cognitive intelligence
it is the waves of our emotional intelligence and
ultimately it is the spiritual intelligence
for it is through the radiance of our spiritual intelligence
that we can attain the 'Godhood ' of Love.

Notes

'Your mere presence' – is a tribute to my late father who occasionally comes in my dreams.

'To Kavita – a poetry of life' is a tribute to my wife. When I was away from her for nine months in Germany I wrote a few lines every week. Also as a tribute to Poetry itself, for I was then trying my hand at writing poems. Kavita means a poem.

Resurrection - My cousin brother's 2nd daughter was married and she died a 'dowry death', presumably burnt by spraying kerosene on her a few years ago!

'Birth of a mother' – a tribute to my late aunty.

A Farmer boy – a version appeared in Poets International Jl. (Ed. M. Fakhruddin), Vol. 9, No. 12, March 1995.

Kavita – a version appeared in Poets International's Anthology '95- 'Golden Thoughts' (Ed. M. Fakhruddin), Aug. 1995.

Re-birth? - first appeared in Camp Fest 1995, Souvenir, NAL, Bangalore, Dec. 1995.

Father - first appeared in Poets International Jl. (Ed. M. Fakhruddin). Vol. 11, No. 2, Feb. 1996.

Space – a version first appeared in Poets International's POETRY 2000 A.D.-World Poetry Anthology (Ed. M.

Fakhruddin), Aug. 1996.

One more ray of hope – a version appeared in Poets International Jl. (Ed. M. Fakhruddin), Vol. 11, No. 8, Aug. 1996.

Mother – first appeared in Poets International's World Poetry Anthology '97- 'Love and Peace' (Ed. M. Fakhruddin), Aug. 1997.

Mid-air wish - first appeared in 'Hansavani', A Home Jl. of NAL, Oct. 1997.

Fighting- a version appeared in Camp Fest '97 Souvenir, NAL, Bangalore, Dec. 1997.

In the village: first appeared in Poets International's Contemporary Poets, 1998.

All the poems in this book are written by me. However, as I vaguely remember, in 'Floods', 'Ruins of the world', 'Beginning...', and 'War kills more ...', some traces/ thoughts from similar titles (of which the authors and the origins were not known to me even at that time - around 1994) that I might have read (in the form of prose-passages and incomplete broken poems) could be found – JIRARA.

The poems "Shiva's cosmic dance", 'Where and what is God?', 'Rebirth', 'Musk deer' and 'Seek Almighty' are reminiscences of my (earlier) belief in God. Due to very strong entrenchment of the concept and philosophy of God in our minds and brains it is difficult to think otherwise. After my expanded reading of science and evolution, I tend to think that there might not be anything like God (as we conventionally believe in many religions). Whether we believe in God or not, and whether God exists of not, we do exist. We 'see' and 'feel' the entire Cosmos through science, and we 'see' and 'feel' the complex biological existence (biological species - inclusive of humans) through evolution. Only if we can feel the pulse of true love (at least through the help of our parents and philosophy), then that is the essence of our lives and in our living – JIRARA.

The poetry 'Seek Almighty' is profusely inspired by and is based on 'Bhaj Govindam' by Bhagwan Shree Shankaracharya ($\sim$ 7th-9th Century A.D.) and the commentary by Swami Chinmayananda (Published by Chinmaya Publications Trust, 175, Rasappa Chetty Street, Chennai, India, some thirty years ago). It is not claimed that the 'Seek Almighty' is equivalent to or can replace the 'Bhaj Govindam'. However, it can be read independent, in the first place, of the original 'Bhaj Govindam'. The first set of lines in 'Seek Almighty' is due to Swamy Chinmayananda (SC) and the second verse is due to Brahmacharini Sharada (BS), and these are included for the sake of completion followed by the poetry by the author (JIRARA).

The poems 'Worship', 'True Prayer', 'God (Bhagavan)', 'Glimpses of Gods of Hindus' are inspired by the literature (in Hindi language) from Shree Shree Ravishankarji. For full description of various Gods and their meanings and significance, please see: Art of God Symbolism by Swamy Chinmayananda, 1987, Central Chinmaya Mission Trust, Powai Park-Drive, Mumbai-400 072.

Poem 'In my rhythm' is inspired by the songs sung by Yesudas, the Indian playback singer with classical, profound and melodious voice.

Expanded notes and Glossary

In Hindu mythology and religion we come across several Gods, some could be historical great humans of principles and role-models and some signify, indicate or define certain principles, good values of life and good characteristics. Many such 'Gods' in Hindu/Indic literature and philosophy are basically some concepts. Like total intellect/intelligence in the Cosmos is considered as a God-principle. Though many deities are human-like Gods, they have to have super qualities (like Rama- Purushottam meaning the best human being) and so on. Though there are, it may look like, thousands of Gods in the Hindu-belief, many have such special meanings, some are representative of several things/objects in the Nature, some represent good and nobler qualities and some indicate highest virtues. Some historical stories and parables are woven around them, and some Gods are portrayed to have had more human-like qualities. Thus, Hindu Gods are not fantasies, or madness, and although they all might not be factual, these Gods in one or other way, or in several ways signify and represent a few or more good qualities that we humans should have (or cultivate) so that the common man, the layperson is continually guided to live good, dutiful and nobler life. It is because of this that these Gods, are even personified and made more like humans with superb characteristics, principles and good values. However, it is then left to the parents, the guardians of our societies, teachers, preachers and philosophers to clarify these aspects to the people at large as to what is really meant to be communicated to them in the greater and deeper sense of the terms Gods and God-hood. So, it is very imperative to realize that Hinduism is necessarily and essentially a philosophy rather than a religion. Its ritualistic practices have some deeper connotations and these do not prevent any body from following only the philosophical route. The Hindu/Indic philosophy, perhaps, can be safely regarded as one of the best and profound philosophies of the world, it suggests a profound way of 'life' rather than way of 'living'. In an abstract sense it being a philosophy, it could be studied, analyzed, ascertained, followed and assimilated by any human being, irrespective of her/his religious beliefs. To follow the associated religious practices is an individual choice or conventions/preferences as and if suggested by a particular society/community for its members.

Some terms found in the 'Seek Almighty' and other (related) poems are explained below. These are often found in the literature on Hindu/Indic philosophy and related spiritual commentaries. Basically these are philosophical aspects and suggest or signify certain profound principles.

Atma – In Hindu mythology/philosophy it is considered as a God principle that is assumed to live in every human being. It points to the soul of humans. It is considered a singleton of the Paramatma, the Universal God principle. Atmagnyana signifies the self-knowledge.

The Universal God Principle is often and variously described as Almighty, Absolute Truth, Truth, Absolute Reality, Bhrahaman, Lord, Absolute Unitary Being,

Paramatma, Eternal Principle, Supreme Being, Eternal Reality in Indic Philosophy.

Bhaja – to sing (glory of God, a deity), to seek the truth

Bhagavan (God) – Bha-ga-v-a-n is the concept as follows:

> Bha – is taken from Bhumi (Earth/solidity)
> ga – is taken from Agni (fire)
> va – is taken from Vayu (air/gas)
> a – is taken from Apasu (water) and Akash (sky/space)

Thus the word Bhagavan represents a collective concept of five elements: Earth, fire, air, water and space

Bhagat – a person who sings devotional songs and is more to ritual practices of the religion

Bhagavat Geeta, Geeta – a sacred book of the Hindu philosophy with 18 chapters, actually describes the duties of an individual and how to live the given life and can be considered as one of the most profound text books on the Indic philosophy. It is the essence of all the Upanishads describing the essence of life, and the methods to achieve the Goal, the true purpose of the life. Its study is quite an intellectual exercise requiring an intense attention.

Bhoga – the enjoyment of life and its pleasures from physical objects

Ganesh – (Lord Ganesh) from Gana – meaning society, collection of people, Isha – meaning head of the society, the Samsar. The word signifies the true leader of the people, society, or community

The Ganges, the chain of Ganga rivers – The Ganges is here meant to be flowing much higher than the human intellectual methods, was brought down (by Lord Shiva) to flow on the Earth that is to the level of the man's experiences. It is also meant to signify that the Ganges flows out of the pure intellect (of Lord Shiva), this pure knowledge flows in the country (India) as its heart. The Ganges is thus the spiritual knowledge (at least for the Hindus). The sanctity of the waters of the Ganges is in its symbolism to signify the spiritual knowledge, the dynamism of the knowledge. The main idea of attaching such an importance is that the people should keep the waters clean and crystal clear, so the waters are available for one and all for drinking. It also signifies that the spiritual knowledge flows from the teacher to the taught, and the pilgrimage to such a holy river, reminds the devotees of their duties and to gain the spiritual wisdom. The ordinary folk, the layman and laywoman not being able to grasp the difficult messages from the Upanishads, Geeta, and so on, due to their illiteracy, ignorance, the lack of background, could be tied to the spiritual knowledge and importance only through the method of giving significance and importance to such objects like river. Similar arguments hold for the art of God symbolism, since for the ordinary persons to understand the philosophical truth is very difficult and they might waste their life times in just mundane works and jobs and just enjoyments, and might contact diseases being lazy or in over indulgence and hence for them to be happy and derive the real joy of the life, during their short span on the planet, the philosophical truths, tenets are conveyed via methods which are easy for them to appreciate and still they can live their lives happily and peacefully, and feel satisfied, gratified that they could do something in their lives. Such methods are conveyed to them via the principle of God and the ritualistic practices, the prayers to the Lord being another such device. Thus, for the ordinary humans the Hathayoga (the practice of hard life, yogasanas, physical exercises, tapas, etc.), the Bhaktiyoga (the singing of devotional songs, prayers, puja, japa, etc.), and Karmayoga (the worship through work, law of action, work principle) are prescribed for their uplift to the higher goals of life and liberation-in-life. For the ones who can understand the philosophical tenets easily the Gnyanayoga (Knowledge Yoga) is prescribed. These prescribed methods are well entrenched in Hindu-philosophical literatures, and are continually upgraded to suit the times of the changing lives and changing times, but with the fundamental tenets still having the same importance and vigor, and are very universal, even if they belong to the Hindu-philosophy, since any one can practice these methods, irrespective of his/her religion-bend of mind, considering these approaches as the means of living a better, and a fulfilled life, and who on this Earth does not want to live such a life?

Godadi – a quilt made from the discarded and thrown away pieces of the clothes, these pieces are just stitched or joined together with self-effort and used for covering the body

Govindam, Govinda – The God, the chosen deity, the Personal God. In a larger sense it points to the Paramatma

Gnyan – the knowledge, not only the superficial information, but complete knowledge

Japa – is a repeated chanting of a chosen Mantra, or devotional verse to gain concentration, to quiet the mind and withdraw the thoughts from the objects of the world and to redirect them to the Almighty. It signifies the enquiry and reflection consisting of discrimination between the permanent and impermanent, repeated pre-thinking, training of the mind such that the mind/thoughts become steady and gain the capacity of understanding the subtler and deeper suggestions of the Scriptures and the philosophical concepts and methods.

Jiva – the soul (of an individual person)

Jivanmukta – obtaining the liberation-in-life, getting freedom from the birth-death cycle

Kali – Goddess so named. Portrayed as a powerful woman with sword, and fear-creating form, and signifies the one who can destroy the bad and evil people.

Karma – the actions (relates to the law of action/Karma)

Krishna (Krsna, Krshna) – A historical God in the Indian epic Mahabharata

Moha – delusion, attachment to the objects of the world and to the kith and kin

Murari – the destroyer of the ego (Mura)

Paramatma – the Universal God principle. It signifies and is conceived as a sum total of all intellect of the entire Cosmos, of which the atman is a sub set-member, a singleton. Thus, the paramatma is a supreme being encompassing all the atmas and jivas in the Cosmos

Pranayama – it is not only the breath control or regulation. Actually it means to have control of five physiological systems: perceptions and reception of things into the subjective life, rejection of things and responses, the digestive system, the circulatory system, capacity to lift ourselves from our present state of understanding to a nobler and highest peak of mountain of knowledge.

Puja (worship) Pu- means completeness, and Ja means get created, happening, become

Rama – Name of one of the historical Gods in Hindu Mythology. Ra – signifies shining, Ma – signifies 'in me', thus, Rama means that shines in me. Rama is the main historical character in the Indian epic Ramayana

Rishi – the Indic traditional term for the accomplished individual who possesses self-knowledge and is well versed in the philosophy of life and living and is adorned by one and all who follow Hindu religion, is regarded as a teacher of the Truth and who might be a Sanyasi

Samsar – The empirical world, the material world where many human relations work (sometimes don't work!), Vishwam also signifies the empirical world full of the people and their mutual relationships

Sanyas, Sanyasi – the total renunciation from the empirical world, the one who has left the world behind him/her and is in the full control of him/her-self.

Sadhu – a derived meaning from Sanyasi, more engaged in the devotional and ritualistic practices of the religion, possesses knowledge of some scriptures
Shastras - the Hindu scriptures

Sahasranamam – the Lord Vishnu has several names, he is also Lakshmipati, husband of wealth (Lakshmi), the wealth as such is regarded as a Goddess

Shiva - the destroyer of the bad world.

Shunya - the 'zero', the naught, nothingness, total annihilation, the vacuum

Tapas – sacrifices, not ordinary charities, but involved ones, with a real aim to attain the Godhood

Vasanas – the desires to possess the objects of the world and to derive pleasures from these objects including the wine, women and wealth

Vishnu – (Lord Vishnu) regarded as the maintainer of the world. One of the trinity Gods of the Hindu mythology: Bhrama, Vishnu and Mahesh (or Shiva). The first one is believed to have created the Universe. The third one is believed to be destroyer of the world. It is believed that there are three major aspects in the world: creation, maintenance and eventual destruction. Each aspect is represented by and attributed to a respective one of the trinity Gods.

Yama – the God-principle of death, the destroyer of the life, the Lord of death, signifies the evolutionary cycle of birth and death of biological species. There is a profound significance to the annihilation and 'creation' in the philosophy. The question of change arises in the realm of death, the change is experienced through the body, mind, and intellect. One who has transcended himself/herself through the process of Yoga, the method of spiritual exercises, then he/she is beyond the realm of death. This is to mean that he/she also dies, but lives the life without fear of death.

Yogi - the Sanyasi, the one who has renounced everything in this word, who has joined himself/herself to the absolute Truth.

Comments from some readers

I really enjoyed your poetry. It was a real surprise
to me to know that you write such beautiful poems -
touching the mind and brain, really great!
- Prof. MR Kaimal University of Kerala, Trivandrum.

Your poems make beautiful reading and I think have
so much depth that one reading is not enough but
many more.
-Dr. Mrs. Girija Gopalratnam, Sc-G, Dy. Director, NAL,
Bangalore.

Well, the poet writes so well.
– Mrs. Padma Madhuranath, Sc-G, Dy. Director, NAL,
Bangalore.

I found 'Birth of a mother' fascinating because of
the way in which the speaker seems to accept her
destiny without any question. She also seems to be
able to look at her own life as if she were an onlooker
and see all the facets of it in one glimpse. There is no
overt sadness at the thought of becoming a mother
and a widow almost at the same time.
- Ms. Barbara English, Pretoria, South Africa.

Very nice poems – Ms. Radhika and Mayur
(Management specialists/small-film makers),
Bangalore.

Very nice poetry and you really write very well - Harshakumari H. Gohil (Children's educational aids specialist), Canada.

'Sweet warm home': The smallest of houses have the biggest of hearts – Ms. Radhika.

'One more ray of hope' a tribute to love, has some very fine piece of poetry -Prof. C. S. Srinivas, Bangalore.